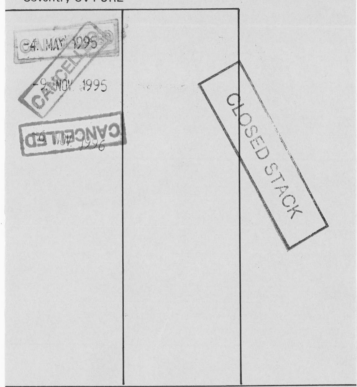

PRINTED AND MADE IN GREAT BRITAIN

ROBES OF THESPIS

Costume Designs by Modern Artists

Edited

for

Rupert Mason

by

George Sheringham

and

R. Boyd Morrison

ERNEST BENN LIMITED

London, Bouverie House

1928

DEDICATED TO

ELLEN TERRY, G.B.E.

WHOSE

LIFE AND GENIUS

HAVE

ENRICHED THE WORLD

vi

SIR WILLIAM ORPEN, K.B.E., R.A.
" The First Costume."

PREFACE

The title of this book is "Robes of Thespis" but its sub-title might well be " The Dawn of Opportunity," for that is precisely the idea which was in my mind when first I considered the possibilities which lie hidden between the covers of such a volume as this.

To bring to light unknown artists—to enable them to have a chance of success hitherto denied them—to prevent their genius, their enthusiasm, from dying before development—to create means of allowing their imagination to have free play—these aims seemed to me worthy of every effort I could command.

But naturally to publish the work of unrecognised artists alone would not create the public interest which was essential to the idea. I sought, therefore, the help of eminent men in art and letters, whose names would give a special value to the book and ensure the wide circulation necessary for the success of the scheme. With some I placed commissions to produce designs specially for this book, and from others I purchased drawings and designs hitherto unpublished; leading men of letters have written special essays on subjects of which they are the acknowledged masters, and among these illustrious ones are found the names and selected works of many not yet famous, but in whom can be discerned the talent which may carry them far. To these has been given the opportunity of public recognition and ultimate success. And so this book is issued with confidence that it may prove a source of pleasure to the connoisseur, of value to the artistic public, of advantage to those who seek reliable information on a subject of absorbing interest, and of real assistance to the younger artists whose well-being I have at heart.

The whole of the profits, which I hope will be considerable, will be devoted to the creation of a fund to help those for whose sake the idea was first advanced.

RUPERT MASON.

ACKNOWLEDGMENT

Mr. Rupert Mason desires to express his grateful thanks to the following for their kind assistance :—

Mr. Fenwick Cutting.
Mr. Martin Hardie, R.E., of The Victoria and Albert Museum.
Mr. P. G. Konody.
Mr. William Nicholson.
Mr. Glyn Philpot, R.A.
Mr. Alan Parsons.
Mrs. Wilcox.
Mr. R. H. Wilenski.

CONTENTS

LIST OF PLATES

LIST OF PLATES

HISTORIC OR "PERIOD" COSTUME—*Continued*

IRISH DRAMATIC COSTUME

COSTUME

COSTUME—*Continued*

COSTUME AT THE LYRIC THEATRE, HAMMERSMITH

LIST OF PLATES

LIST OF PLATES

I
FANTASY IN COSTUME

C

FANTASY IN COSTUME
POINTS RAISED BY AN OPERA HAT

By Max Beerbohm

I used to live in London. I was even born there. I took the whole place as a matter of course. But now I live more than six hundred miles away from it; and my visits to it are as those of a simple, gaping, alien sight-seer. A note of scarlet is struck by the Baedeker that I bear through your grey thoroughfares.

I was last there in the Spring of 1925; and one of the sights made a quite ineffaceable impression on me, though I had but a glimpse of it. I was in a taxi-cab, and had asked the driver to go quickly as I was late for dinner at a friend's house. Through the open window of my vehicle I saw thus only for an instant my old friends, those two distinguished brothers in art, Charles Ricketts and Charles Shannon, walking together, and though I waved my hand wildly to them they did not see me. At any rate, Shannon did not. Ricketts may have, perhaps, and just ignored me. For I was not wearing a top-hat. And Ricketts was.

I saw him with it on. Moreover, it was an opera hat—a gibus, a chapeau-bras—a thing that opens with a loud plop and closes with a quiet snap; old-world emblem of the frivolous and the mundane, the light and worthless.

Wondrous enough to me, on the fine head of Ricketts, would have been a top-hat for use by daylight only. Thirty years ago everybody, except Ricketts, and with him Shannon, sometimes wore a hat of that kind. Indeed, most of us wore such hats all the time—while we were within the four-mile radius and out of doors. Only in August, and in the earlier weeks of September, did the average man dare to be seen wearing in the metropolis a hat

3

of straw or felt. At other seasons, unless one were driving to a railway-terminus, with some luggage on the roof of the cab, such head-gear marked one out as something of an anarch. It seemed to be lacking in respect to Queen Victoria, though she herself was so seldom in our midst. When her son came to the throne, the top-hat began to totter upon our heads. He, after all, was a man : no question of chivalry was involved. Top-hats were rather heavy and hot. The heathen in their blindness bowed down to felt and straw. But they were conscious that this was not a right form of worship. Now they have lost altogether their decent misgivings. Nay, many of the younger ones worship nothing at all: they go about hatless, carrying high in the eyes of all beholders heads naked of aught but hair, without interference by the police. Oh for the less spacious times of great Victoria ! But vain are the heart-cries of the fogey. The top-hat, so appropriate to the character of a London that is vanishing now—a Londonish, an unprovincialised and unamericanised London—is to all intents and purposes gone, extinct, hardly rememberable. The top-hat is never worn by anybody, except Ricketts. Not even by Shannon. And yet—I won't despair of Shannon. It is many years since he joined the Royal Academy, suddenly. And Ricketts was separable. He followed his friend only the other day. Perhaps I shall see Shannon in a top-hat yet.

I wonder, does Ricketts wear that collapsible crown of his only when he dines out? Or does he, when he comes home, close it with a quiet snap and place it under his pillow, ready for the first thing in the morning? Some painters wear hats when they are working, to shade their eyes. Does Ricketts at his easel wear his gibus? It would seem to me incongruous with his canvas. He is sensitively keen on many periods in the world's history; but I have never noted in his work any trace of absorption in the manners of Victoria's time : his mind ranges further back and wider afield. The rigid top-hat is at any rate a thing of the Regency; and so late as in the eighteen-fifties any gentleman attending an evening party glided into the drawing-room with that hat in his left hand, and was not parted from it. The gibus is a mere mushroom. I would even call it a toadstool, for it is redolent of that sinister thing, the growth of machinery—our world's blight and curse. An ingenious little machine it is, I grant you. I can enjoy the plop and the snap of it myself. But its charm is not comparable with that of the top-hat proper. It can play its two tricks, but it has no moods. It cannot be rubbed the wrong way. It doesn't care how you treat it. And its nature is dull, sombre. It never comes radiant from the iron, flashing broadly back the single light of the sun, or narrowly back as many artificial lights as may be cast upon it; whereas—

But I cannot make the juvenile reader share my faded old enthusiasm. He derides me as a praiser of the pot at the expense of the kettle. His desire is for colour and for fantasy. That is very natural. In about 1830 there was inaugurated (for men only) a tyranny of black and white and grey, and of austere prosaicism in form. In about 1910 there was at last a slight and

PLATE I

MAX BEERBOHM

Here are five friends of mine—Mr. Nicholson, Mr. Rutherston, Mr. Craig, Mr. Morrison, and Mr. Ricketts. All are designers of fantastic and lovely costumes. Yet, they dress themselves thus:—

Here are five friends of mine
— Mr. Nicholson, Mr. Rutherston, Mr.
Craig, Mr. Morrison, and Mr. Ricketts.
All are designers of fantastic and
lovely costumes. Yet they
themselves dress
thus:—

timid reaction. Socks and ties were often quite vivid, until, in 1914, the great tidal wave of khaki overwhelmed them. At the withdrawal of that they re-appeared, these details, and were welcomed. In 1925 there was, I perceived, even a touch of fantasy. The Oxford trousers and the "pull-over" were a step in the right direction; but a slight step and the only one. I applaud the young men's desire for fantasy and colour. I do but wish they would show more inclination to satisfy it. To all intents and purposes, the aspect of the streets of London is no more enlivened by men's costume than it was when first I knew it. Only on the stages of some theatres do fantasy and colour, for both sexes, abound and thrive.

True fantasy is a rather recent thing there. In pantomimes and ballets there was always some fantasy, of course; but it was of a perfunctory and stale order. In Shakespearean and other "costume" plays there never was any stint of colour, and the colours were often lovely; but fantasy was barred, in costumes as in scenery. Gordon Craig started the revolt, design-ing costumes, as he designed scenery, rather from his inward fancy than by recourse to facts. The designing of theatrical clothes became a creative art. Ricketts, William Nicholson, Albert Rutherston, Dulac, Glyn Philpot, George Sheringham, Boyd Morrison, and other gifted men, have revelled in it. Of course, what the actors and actresses wear is not really quite so important as what they say and how they say it. A very dowdily-dressed performer, speaking lines that are worth hearing, and speaking them in such a way that they can be heard by people who have not obtained seats in the front row of the stalls, will achieve a greater success than can be hoped for by a most divinely clad rival who does otherwise. Still this rival cuts a fine figure, and the hearts of the audience glow with gratitude to the designer of the wondrous effect. "And," says the audience to itself, "art-ists are notoriously vain and selfish. If this designer can thus glorify others, what must his own raiment be !" And at the fall of the curtain there arises a loud cry, "Designer ! Designer !" The call is not taken. The cry per-sists, rising to a key of anger. The manager comes on, rather pale, to say that the designer is "not in the house." The manager, believe me, is a liar. The designer is there, right enough, but he dares not show himself. You ask me why he is so diffident? Really I haven't time to give a verbal explanation of a matter so subtle. I will do a drawing.

I have done the drawing.* Dulac I had to omit, for it is ten years since I had the pleasure of meeting him, and he may have metamorphosed in the meantime. There was just a touch of romanticism in his costume (as there was also in that of the lamented Lovat Fraser), but the colouring was sternly subdued : black and darkest grey were the notes. Glyn Philpot is not here, because I find his face very difficult to portray. As to his clothes, I assure you that no conclave of the soberest pundits of Savile Row would find one point in them for deprecation. I have given Ricketts the small sombrero that I had always associated with him. When one does a drawing, what is

* Reproduced opposite page 4.

5

one glimpse as against the vision of a lifetime? I thought I might brighten the group by giving Nicholson a canary-coloured waistcoat. But sincerity forbade. It is many years since he ceased to strike that note of colour for us. Albert Rutherston eschewed, from the very outset of his career, aught that is conspicuous in hue or fashion. George Sheringham is equally discreet. So is Boyd Morrison. Craig at one time used to wear no necktie, but always wears one nowadays. Also, he wears the overcoat that you see here, in preference to his cloak. And was the cloak itself extraordinary, after all? Not really, when one comes to think of it. Painters and poets had been wearing such cloaks throughout the Victorian Era. The young gentlemen of the Quartier Latin were wearing them, as we all know, in the days of Gavarni. Why should mere sleevelessness be the symbol of revolt against the established order of things? Why don't our rebels invent new symbols, as they go on? A black cloak, with a black sombrero—surely this eternal formula cannot for ever satisfy the insurgent soul of youth and genius. In France it certainly doesn't. The students in Paris do ever run changeful riot in corduroy, velvet, and all manner of fabrics, dyed in all manner of colours. There is evidently some deep-rooted national difference—something that inhibits our rebels in their wish to look rebellious, and tones down to a timorous gloom the expression of their ardours. Even that brightness of ties and socks which quite conventional young men dare to indulge in is beyond their range. It is all very sad. What is to to be done about it?

I appeal to the designers of theatrical costumes. Doubtless they have hoped that the orgies of colour and fantasy with which they grace the theatres would have a marked effect on the streets, instead of merely making the streets' effect duller than ever by contrast. I suggest to these eminent friends of mine that they should design costumes not merely for actors and actresses, but also for citizens. I hear them murmur that there would be no demand for these, but I am not deterred. Let them, I say, make the demand themselves. Let them go around setting the example. This is a splendid idea. I am too excited to write about it. I will do another drawing.

I have done the drawing.* It rather disappoints me. But it might be worse. I need hardly explain that the costumes are entirely haphazard. I didn't attempt (I was too excited) to do designs characteristic of the men drawn. I just clothed them hurriedly in anything bright that occurred to me. Only once did I pause. I was about to give Ricketts an opera hat of many colours. But this would have been to carry fantasy too far; and I curbed my foolish pencil.

* Reproduced on opposite page.

PLATE II

MAX BEERBOHM
" Why Not Rather Thus ? "

PLATE III

EDWARD GORDON CRAIG
" Hamlet."   An Actor.   Act II.   Scene 2.

ege
1910

Hamlet.
An Actor.
act. II scene. 2.

PLATE IV

GLADYS SPENCER CURLING
"Seraphina."

PLATE V

GLADYS SPENCER CURLING
" Fantasy in Silver."

PLATE VI

CECIL FFRENCH SALKELD
"Warrior."

PLATE VI

CECIL FFRENCH SALKELD
" Warrior."

PLATE VII

CECIL PFRENCH SALKELD
" Bride."

PLATE VIII

EDMUND DULAC
" The Mycenaean Dancer."
For " Phi-Phi," Musical Comedy.

PLATE IX

EDMUND DULAC
" Meander."
For " Phi-Phi," Musical Comedy.

PLATE X

EDMUND DULAC
"Dancer."
For "Phi-Phi", Musical Comedy

PLATE X

EDMUND DULAC
" Dancer."
For " Phi-Phi," Musical Comedy.

PLATE XI

EDMUND DULAC
" Faun."
For " Phi-Phi," Musical Comedy.

PLATE

ALBERT WETHERSTON
"mes"

PLATE XIII

LUCY NORTON
" The Maiden."

d'arcy horton

II
HISTORIC OR "PERIOD" COSTUME

HISTORIC OR "PERIOD" COSTUME;
WITH SPECIAL REFERENCE TO THE WORKS OF SHAKESPEARE

By Francis M. Kelly

Only the other day, so to speak, at the King's Theatre, Hammersmith, Sir Barry Jackson introduced us to a " Hamlet " in all the trappings of the year of Grace, 1925. The experiment, from a certain point of view a *reductio ad absurdum*, appears to have created a mild sensation. My own views upon this method of production are of no particular consequence, nor are they relevant to the theme of the present essay: the evolution of stage costume from Shakespeare's times to the present day. Yet, if I know myself, I shall be surprised if they do not erupt sporadically as this chapter continues.

It is, of course, not claimed within present limits to offer a full and complete account of what would by itself suffice to fill a goodly tome. The necessary material exists beyond question. To sift and digest it with any degree of thoroughness, to present it afterwards at once fully and lucidly, would require considerable leisure and prolonged study; the more so that the literature of the subject is a very scattered one, and has never been extracted from its context and brought into a coherent whole. It may be, however, that the following paper will, if only by its imperfections, stimulate a worthier pen to essay the task and to present us with a more searching and comprehensive study.

In Shakespeare's day, we are constantly reminded, the actor trod the boards in the ordinary dress of the period. Now this statement, true enough *in the main*, should not be made without qualifications. To these we shall have occasion to refer presently. In the meantime, having in principle admitted that Shakespeare's heroes and heroines made their first bow to the public apparelled according to the contemporary fashions, it may be not impertinent to pause and consider what the distinctive features of these fashions were; for the plays contain a number of allusions to the costume of the day, which to the average modern ear are meaningless—as no doubt they have been from about the Restoration down to the present, despite the admirable work of the commentators. Compared with many of his contemporaries, Shakespeare is rather chary of such allusions; but they are more numerous and definite than is generally supposed. Even writers on costume appear to have underrated their importance and number.[1]

Having then to some extent explained in what the actor's attire agreed with that of his audience, we will try to see what features, if any, were peculiar to the stage. The widely scattered contemporary references to our subject await methodic collation, while delineations of actors " in character " are seemingly all but unknown in England prior to the XVIIIth century. However, it is possible to gather much collateral information from the writings of contemporary men of letters such as Greene, Nashe, Marston, Gosson, Ben Jonson, Beaumont and Fletcher, etc.), on the one hand, on the other from Henslowe's diary and papers, the accounts of the Office of the Revels and similar records.

The principal items of men's attire in Shakespeare's day (I am taking as his period of activity the years 1591–1613, as given by the " Encyclopædia Britannica," eleventh edition, under " Shakespeare ") were the *doublet* and *hose*. The former was a close-fitting jacket, high necked and long-waisted, the waistline generally sloping to a V-shaped point in front. The skirts were mostly quite short, the sleeves might be either tight-fitting, or loose (of a " bishop " or " leg of mutton " shape), but caught in close at the wrist. Fashionable folk commonly stiffened out the doublet with busks and bombast (—padding) and between c. 1575–95 exquisites stuffed the belly into a great overhanging paunch *à la* Punchinello. Subsequently, from about 1605, there was a vogue for a corset-like, rigid form compressing the waist to wasp-like slimness. At this date the term hose may apply to breeches and stockings united, or to the former only; it is not always possible to decide which. Breeches and stockings, formerly combined in one, were now rapidly becoming independent articles. The breeches presented many varieties of cut; the extremes of contrast being marked by the *trunk-hose* (trunk breeches, t. slops, trunks) on the one hand and the *venetians* on the other. Trunk-hose (referred to by Shakespeare as " French hose," "French slop," " round hose," " short blistered breeches ") were short breeches of disproportionate width, often grotesquely distended with horsehair, flocks,

---

[1] E.g. Calthrop ("English Costume"), who has devoted a section to Shakespeare's references to dress, and the late Percy McQuoid in his chapter on costume in " Shakespeare's England."

bran, etc. They always stopped some inches short of the knee, and unless
" long-stocked " (i.e., having long stockings sewn direct to them) had
" canions " (tubular extensions to the knee) allowing of independent stockings being worn with them. *Venetians*, or " long hose " (not mentioned by
Shakespeare, any more than are trunk-hose,—but of frequent occurrence
in inventories and wardrobe accounts, civilian and theatrical, to say nothing
of contemporary literature) reached to below the knee where they were
tied or buttoned and were normally fairly close in fit. *Gaskins* mentioned
in "Twelfth Night," I. v. 27 (gally-hose, galligaskins, gally-slops are presumably identical or similar), if they be anything more than a generic term,
appear to have been some sort of wide knickers intermediate between the
two last described forms. Over the doublet was often worn a *jerkin*, or over-
jacket, of which there were several varieties—cassocks, jackets, coats,
frocks, mandilions—long or short, tight or loose, with or without sleeves.
In addition there was a variety of cloaks, some scarce reaching the hip,
others hanging to the calf. Some had falling collars behind, some had up-
right collars and lapels, others were collarless or furnished with hanging
cowls. Elderly and professional men preferred gowns,[1] generally with
hanging sleeves, a feature found also in jerkins and cloaks. About the necks
both sexes wore great cartwheel ruffs set in tubular pleats, starched and
supported on wires, while the men also affected falling bands : i.e., small turn
down collars of lawn or lace. The gallant of this date was surmounted by a
tall bag-shaped cap (rare after about 1595), a high sugar-loaf hat ("copatain"
" Taming of the Shrew," V. i. 69), or a spreading sombrero, and shod with
tight, slashed shoes or (less commonly) closely-fitting boots. Shoe-roses
and heels are not found till about 1600. The great majority of chins were
bearded.

Meanwhile the ladies' attire was no less typical of the age. Their bodices
and corsets were even more mercilessly tight-laced than those of the men.
Their general use of paint and false hair, with the variety of its dressing,
their veils, coifs, French hoods, wired out or hanging sleeves clamour for
notice separately; to say nothing of the various items they filched from
their men-folk. In addition to the various ruffs and falling bands worn by
the latter, the women had a number of forms of neckwear all their own.
Their grand invention was the *verdingale*, or farthingale, whether the Spanish funnel-shaped form or the drum-like French variety. The first was a
crinoline-like hooped under-petticoat, the second a great padded roll put
about the hips beneath the petticoat. The abrupt contrast between the
tightly compressed torso and monstrous hips is compared by Henri
Estienne to a rod stuck in the centre of a tree trunk. Of all these
particulars much could be written, but we should find ourselves
carried too far. It has all been described more or less completely,
and the intending student may be profitably referred to the passages in

---

[1] To omit the cloak or gown in public (to go *in cuerpo*, as it was termed) was accounted
"bad form."

question.[1] Meanwhile, let us proceed without further ado to the professional attire of the actor when Shakespeare's plays were first "put on."

Now, whether we peruse the accounts of the Office of the Revels, or the professional inventories, diaries, etc., of theatrical managers like Henslowe, we meet at every turn with the usual articles of civil attire already described. It seems clear that these are essentially the same as those to be found " in front of the house," or in the streets outside. There may have been a touch of garishness which jarred upon a more sensitive taste (*e.g.*, in colour and trimmings), a note of cheapness or flashiness. But though there are costumes or properties apparently adapted to particular characters, in general the items are practically indistinguishable from what one meets in ordinary civil documents such as wills, etc. Certainly the bright colours and showy trimmings of these theatrical wardrobes seem to contrast with the restrained colour-scheme and tasteful decoration that we meet with in Elizabethan portraits (under James I. this restraint and good taste change for the worse). Yet it would be a mistake to think of them as merely tawdry. We note that despite occasional reference to " *counterfet* cloth of golde," " coper lace " (doubtless in lieu of real gold lace), "counterfeit morions," etc., the wardrobes of at least the better-class companies consisted largely of costly materials : velvet, silk, satin, etc. And this splendour of apparel on the London stage is confirmed in various independent quarters. Whether as the joint property of the fellowship or the personal belongings of the individual comedian, stage-dresses and properties were the chief vehicle of theatrical display and the actors' most valuable asset. They might be acquired by gift, bequest or purchase; in particular instances they would be borrowed for the occasion. Actors were apt to fall back upon the resources of the tiring-room in order to make a brave show when they walked abroad. Eventually this provoked so much unfavourable comment on the part of moralists, satirists and others that the thing became a scandal and was eventually prohibited by the authorities. Managers also disapproved of it as an abuse of valuable properties. The old-time actor was ranked officially among " rogues and vagabonds," nor was he allowed to forget it for long. Fynes Moryson brackets actors with " bankrouts " among the riffraff who dare to go about richly attired; although some writers appear to take a kind of vicarious, patriotic pride in the lavishness of our English stage-productions. Nor do native authors only condemn or laud the richness of contemporary theatrical display; foreign visitors, such as the German Thomas Platter, 1595, Prince Lewis of Anhalt, 1596, and Orazio Busino, secretary to the Venetian embassy, 1617–18, are unanimous in

[1] Any of the books cited under B in the Bibliography (p. 32 *infra*) may be consulted with advantage. The author of the present paper described the principal modes of Shakespeare's day in some detail in a series of papers—"Shakespearian Dress-Notes"—for the "Burlington Magazine," 1916–17. Compare accounts and inventories in the Henslowe "Papers" and "Diary" (W. W. Greg's edition) or those of the Office of Revels published by Feuillerat, with the ordinary wills and inventories of the day.

confirmation. In fact in 1613 Olorinus, a German, wishing to condemn the ostentation of his youthful contemporaries, wrote : " Such a brave show was made, that the younger generation walked abroad like English actors upon the stage." Platter explains the " splendour and comeliness " of our stage-apparel, by the statement that it was largely recruited from the effects of defunct noblemen, often bequeathed to lackeys and by them sold to the players.[1]

In 1595 the Vice-Chancellor of Cambridge (Thomas Nevil) approached the Lord Chamberlain with a request to be allowed to borrow " ancient princely attire, which is nowhere to be found but in the Office of the Robes in the Tower " (Brit. Mus. Lansdowne MSS. No. 78). It is more than likely, although we have no evidence on the point, that the request was granted, for at a still later period we find even greater favours conceded to " *the* Profession." Thus when Davenant produced his " Love and Honour " (1661-2?) with the " Duke's Servants " at Lincoln's Inn Fields, we are informed that " it was richly dressed, the King, the Duke of York and the Earl of Oxford having [respectively] given their coronation suits to Betterton [as Prince Alvaro], Harris [Prosper] and Price [Lionel] " — v. " Roscius Britannicus," 1708, by John Downes (sometime prompter to the company). In the same spirit Mary of Modena, when (as Duchess of York) she witnessed Mrs. Elizabeth Barry's performance in the Earl of Orrery's " Mustapha " in 1673, was so delighted that she presented the actress with her own " wedding suit "; and later, when queen to James II., bestowed upon this actress her coronation robes for the part of Queen Elizabeth in Banks' " Earl of Essex." Incidentally it seems not too daring a speculation to assume that some of the costly dresses designed for court-masques found their eventual way into the theatrical tiring room and had their influence on stage-costume. Before leaving this part of our subject it may be worth noting that the actors could and did occasionally earn an extra bit of money by hiring out portions of their wardrobes for weddings and other gala occasions; at a pinch they could raise the wind by pawning them. Apart from ready-made garments, it is worth remarking that even at this date companies would retain a regular tailor to make up into costumes materials bought in the piece.

To come now to the differences between stage-apparel and the dress common to their audience; and here it is to be regretted that our information is sadly defective. We read for instance of " a robe for to goo invisibell," but what stage-convention was accepted by the public as implying invisibility we have no means of guessing. Again we seem to have no very clear

[1] See Chambers, Sir E. K., "The Elizabethan Stage," Clarendon Press, Oxford, 1923, vol. ii, p. 364. The MS. of Platter of Basle's travels, 1595, is in the Basle University Library and quoted in "Anglia," xxii, 456. A propos of the English stage he remarks : "The players are apparelled with the utmost refinement and elegance, for it is customary in England when a gentleman of high rank or a knight dies, to make over and bestow wellnigh his finest apparel to his servants; and these, since it is not seemly for them to wear such raiment, but only to imitate it, hand it over for purchase to the actors at a cheap rate."

indication as to the dress and make-up of a ghost. Mr. Percy Simpson ("Shakespeare's England" II. xxiv. 268) thinks the stage ghost was at least occasionally garbed in leather; although the little evidence he quotes seems hardly conclusive. Incidentally he points out that the ghost of Hamlet's father on the "platform before the castle of Elsinore" is according to the mere text armed ". . . From top to toe?—My lord, from head to foot"; while on the other hand in the scene between Hamlet and his mother the stage direction in the First Folio runs "Enter the ghost in his night gowne" (*i.e.*, dressing gown). To judge merely from Shakespeare's text, stage-kings rarely removed their crowns except when retiring to rest or for purposes of disguise. Cf. the player-king's business in "Hamlet" and the scene in "Henry IV" in which Prince Hal assumes his sleeping father's crown; or the incognito of Polixenes in the "Winter's Tale." Mythical and monstrous beings—I suppose Caliban would come into the latter class —appear to have been distinguished by symbolic trimmings and properties. Thus we read of sea-deities in blue and green robes garlanded with "sea grass" and bearing tridents. Property heads too seem to have been in use, judging not only from inventories, but from old prints.[1] A curious point, considering the numerous battle scenes in plays of this date, is the lack, in such inventories and descriptions as I have met, of arms and armour. Were these simply borrowed as required?[2] Remembering the tendency, even in the regular armies of the day, largely to discard defensive armour, it may well be that a helmet, cuirass, gorget, target or the like were by a tacit convention accepted as representing a càp-a-pié accoutrement. Again, the mention, à propos of a court masque of 1598, of "counterfeit morions" and another of "headpieces of cloth of gold," as also of "bodies of carnation cloth of silver . . . cut to express the naked in the manner of the Greek thorax" suggest that textile materials with a metallic sheen, perhaps stiffened with buckram or pasteboard, were employed to suggest the real thing. It may be worth noting how rare are specific references in Shakespeare and his contemporaries to details of armour. It is perhaps significant that the only specific name for a helmet used by Shakespeare (omitting one reference to the then obsolete *salet*, introduced for the sake of a pun) is the *burgonet*, a semi-open helmet of the period, used for horse and foot, and able to be worn without impeding the actor's utterance.[3]

There is, however, at least one "line" of character on the Elizabethan

[1] See plate 12b in Hartley and Elliott's "Life and Work of the People of England," the sixteenth century; London, Batsford, 1925.
[2] Cf. P. Cunningham: "Extracts from the Accounts of the Revels at Court," 1571-9, pp. 11, 24, 59, 89, 135. Roger Tyndall (member of London Armourers' Guild in 1537, will dated 1581 and proved 1590) seems to have regularly hired out arms and armour for the court-revels. Cf. also Feuillerat's two books (see Bibliography *infra*) on pasteboard property-armour.
[3] Horatio's words (Hamlet II, ii) anent the Ghost :—"He wore his *beaver up*" suggest the ghost having a "close helmet"—Beaver here=visor of face-guard.

stage which appears to have had its distinctive habit : the " clown." The term is used sometimes of the professional " fool" or jester, the distinctive features of whose dress had been handed down by tradition and can be seen in a few sixteenth century paintings.[1]

On the other hand we have the true clown, or, as he would have been termed at a later date, the " comic countryman," the stage-yokel whose uncouth demeanour and broad dialect mask a curious mixture of real cunning with surface simplicity. The actors Tarleton and Kempe were famous exponents of this particular " line." The attire of this character was a highly conventionalised version of that of the garb identified with rustics, probably bearing as much resemblance to its alleged prototype as did the " Zanne " of the Italian *commedia dell' arte* or the " Pierrot " and " Gilles " of the French stage. Although Tarleton's costume, his " great clownish slop " and " buttoned cap," has been referred to by contemporaries, in his one known portrait (a rather coarse drawing, it is true) he figures in a loose belted jacket, *trousers* and bérèt-like cap, with " high-lows " (or " startups " as they were termed) buckled inside the ankle. It is worthy of mention in passing that trousers appear to have been worn to some extent among the peasantry from remote times. Sewn-on patches of various bright colours were a regular feature (hence possibly the old term " patch " for a fool), which developed eventually into the patchwork costume still worn by Harlequin. Or again, in his character of "innocent" or half-wit, the clown sometimes appeared in a long piebald gown. Tarleton, by the way, is said to have affected grey or brown in his apparel. Almost his contemporary on the French stage was Robert Guérin, better known as Gros-Guillaume, who played analogous parts in a costume of the same type.

As opposed to the " low comedy " rustic, we also have the more idyllic swain, the shepherd of Arcady to balance the Bœotian. Wreaths of flowers, and sheep or goat skins appear, with a crook, to have distinguished the genus. Rosalind in the forest of Arden, disguised as " Ganymede," Perdita as the shepherd's adopted child are of this particular unreal family. Pastoral poems vaguely based upon Theocritus and his like were much in vogue. The " Aminta " of Tasso, Guarini's " Pastor Fido," Sidney's " Arcadia " had popularised a world of romantic pseudo-shepherds, whose counterparts are to be found in France in d'Urfé's " Astrée," in Spain in Montemayor's much-translated " Diana." How little relation these " shepherds " bore to the real thing may be judged not only by the high falutin dialogue allotted to them, but also by their apparel, which as often as not was of cloth of gold or bright coloured silk. Leone de Sommi would have his pastoral characters in " fleshings," or even, when young and of fine figure, bare-limbed. D'Urfé in his " Astrée " (1618) says : " Such as play the part of shepherds on the stage are by no means attired in coarse materials, wooden clogs or ill-cut suits as actually worn by our countryfolk;

[1] Cf. "Allegorical Love Feast," by P. Pourbus (London, Wallace Collection), and L. van Valckenborch's "Spring Landscape," Vienna Hofmuseum.

15

on the contrary they carry gilt or painted crooks, their clothes are of taffeta, their pouches daintily shaped and oft-times of gold or silver tissue." In some plays however the peasantry was simply enough presented in trousers and startups, draped in a sheepskin and crowned with laurel. Henslowe's wardrobe included white shepherd's costumes, but how cut or of what material is not stated. Many of the alleged " shepherds " differed little in their main lines from the fashionable apparel of the day.

Of appropriate " period " costume there was no understanding, nor did the question at all concern the Shakespearian stage. On the other hand there was to a limited degree an attempt to suggest local colour (irrespective of date) in the case of Turks, " pagans " and extra-European races generally. Theatrical inventories, stage directions and indeed the very titles of certain plays imply as much. Thus the stage direction—" Enter Morochus, a tawny Moor, all in white "—sufficiently differentiates the Prince of Morocco in the " Merchant of Venice " from the other characters. The turban (or " tulbent " as it was called) was by no means unfamiliar to Shakespearian audiences. And here I venture to record my personal conviction that Othello, apart from his " sooty " complexion, should in no way be presented as a " turban'd Turk "; his own contemptuous reference to such an one in his dying speech should definitely settle the question apart from other argument :—

> " . . . . in Aleppo once,
> Where a malignant and a *turban'd Turk*
> Beat a Venetian and traduced the State,
> I took by the throat the *circumcized dog*,
> And smote him—thus ! "

Again, though this time the occasion is a masquerade, in " Love's Labour's Lost," the King and his friends enter in Russian habits, to which there are references elsewhere: these we may assume to have been long, fur-trimmed gowns or caftans, fur caps and high boots. The numerous albums of contemporary costumes so popular in the late sixteenth century,[1] to say nothing of Braun and Hogenberg's " Civitates," would afford models. So would the less familiar " embassages " to this country.

Friars, priests and prelates seem at all times to have worn traditional stock habits more or less in accordance with their character, including tonsured wigs, and in this respect contrast strongly with their surroundings from the seventeenth to the nineteenth century. A good example is the half-length portrait of Lacy (National Portrait Gallery), a favourite actor of Charles II. in "The Spanish Friar." Cf. also the various churchmen in Nicholas Rowe's illustrated Shakespeare of 1709. The same Lacy in the part of " Sawney the Scot," in correct highland garb, is represented in the triple portrait by John Michael Wright at Hampton Court.

[1] Starting with a series of prints by Enea Vico and an anonymous Parisian album published by "Sluperus" in 1562, we get an important series of such books from 1577 onward : Weigel, A. de Bruyn, Boissard, Bertelli, Vecellio, Franco, etc.

We have hitherto avoided particular reference to state-pageants and to the masques so popular at the courts of Elizabeth and James I, although playwrights like Ben Jonson, Marston, Davenant, etc., composed librettos for them, and an Inigo Jones did not disdain to design costumes and settings. While we have suggested that their influence upon the professional stage can hardly be doubted, yet in the lack of definite evidence to fill up beyond cavil the links in the chain, it has appeared better to " play for safety "; merely noting the dances and masques (introducing allegorical and mythological characters) interpolated in more than one of Shakespeare's plays. Before quitting this part of our study, it may be remarked that there is one glaring exception to the indifference that prevailed right into the nineteenth century with respect to correct historical garb and " make-up." Nothing could more strikingly exemplify the indelible impression made upon the people of England by the outward man of Henry VIII, than the fact that, however the other characters in history or in plays have been portrayed, this one figure invariably conforms more or less to Holbein's portraits in " make-up " and dress. Not " good Queen Bess," not " the Martyr King " left so clear cut a recollection. Compare all the illustrations of Shakespeare from Rowe's edition down.

The Restoration does not appear to have brought in any particular improvement worth notice in respect of stage-apparel, despite such concrete expressions of royal good will as we have already noted in respect of Betterton and Mrs. Barry. One cannot, be it said in passing, but dissent from Planché's remarks on the pre-Commonwealth stage, with its " considerable attention . . . paid to the costume of historical or classical personages, and a *laudable desire* . . . to render it *as accurate as possible*." Charles II and his companions in exile had contracted a taste for things French, as in other things so with regard to the stage; as a consequence, not long after the Restoration, Betterton was sent to Paris to study the *mise en scène* employed there and note anything likely in his judgment to be suitable for transference to the English boards. Since there can be little doubt that this visit had tangible effects upon the London theatres, it may be as well to get some notion of the general character of stage-costume under Louis XIV. The court-masques and ballets so beloved of the monarch in his younger years had an immediate and lasting influence upon the professional stage. The costume of the French theatre may be roughly divided into three categories : (1) Roman costume—which includes Greece and indeed all "classical "antique subjects; (2) Turkish, which, with alterations, could be adapted to all " barbarous " or " pagan " themes; (3) modern, *i.e.*, the costume of the period (not merely the period of the original production, but of any revival that might take place within the next century). 1 and 2 were used for tragedy, 3 was employed for comedy. In France, Richelieu may be said to have started a real official patronage of the stage; Louis XIV followed suit, and the Regent and Louis XV (to say nothing of his mistresses) carried on the policy of encouraging the professional stage and taking it under their wing. Marie Antoinette, too, extended her favour to the profession. The result was that, however ridiculous and inappropriate the *mise en scène* might be, it was not restricted by lack of means. In France, even in Molière's time, the costumes were at least not shabby. For the " Roman" costumes the accessories and trimmings must be of genuine, fine gold and silver: firstly, because inferior stuff quickly deteriorated, and secondly, because in the presence of the foppish spectators who lined the stage any sham was at once detected.[1] Even in private life the French actor of the leading town companies had to make a brave show; for he was liable at any time to be summoned to court, and he had to consort with young bloods, who made it a hobby of having prominent members of *the* " profession " in their train; although, as was pointedly shown over Molière's funeral, the actor was liable at every turn to be reminded of his legal status—as a " rogue and vagabond." Even at this date the stage occasionally set the fashion for the town; *e.g.*, the gown called the *audrienne*, first exhibited in Michel Baron's adaptation of Terence's " Andria." It would seem that some of the costumes used by the leading companies often were worth some £300 in pre-war English currency, and that an actor's wardrobe occasionally reached the equivalent of £2,000. In respect of the " tragic " costume, it should be noted that no distinction was known between " Greeks " and " Romans "; also that " Russians " and " Turks " were mixed up in many plays; to say nothing of the admixture of " savage " elements, indicated by fur and feathers. Comedy was played *in the main* in " modern " costume; *i.e.*, in the mode in vogue at the date *of performance*. But even here we have to make certain exceptions. Thus certain plays of Molière—"Amphitryon," " La Princesse d' Élide," " Les Amants Magnifiques "—were played from the outset in " Roman " costume. Even in the ordinary comedies there were certain stock " lines " of character which were always associated with a particular type of dress. In particular the low-comedy part of the resourceful, crafty valet (Scapin, Crispin and Co.) wore a conventional livery derived from the Italian *commedia dell' arte*.

Before returning to our own Restoration stage, it may be well to point out the general characteristics of the French, Viennese (and in general the continental) idea of " Roman " or " tragic " costume. Your tragic " Roman " was distinguished by a *tonnelet*, a species of funnel-shaped, stiffened-out kilt, over which sprawled the festooned lappets of the close-fitted bodice which was intended to reproduce in textiles and embroidery the old Roman military cuirass. At the back hung an elaborately draped cloak, the legs were encased in fleshings and shod in tall buskins with red heels. The whole edifice was topped by a great full-bottomed wig in the latest court-fashion, surmounted by a fantastic helmet or by a lavishly plumed hat. The ladies were very tightly laced and wore bunches of ostrich-feathers over the latest mode in hair-dressing. Long trains were usually worn and the costume was distinguished from that of every day life only by symbolic trimmings

---

[1] Chappuzeau: "Théâtre Français"; Mantzius: "History of Theatrical Art," vol. iv, etc.

and pendant flaps. Amazons, " Indian queens " and the like wore very short skirts and tall, high-heeled boots. Be it noted that at this date, or little later, Bibiena (1657–1743), Burnacini (1636–1707) and A. D. Bertoli (1678–1743) were designing elaborate and costly stage-costumes for the stage in Vienna, which for technical excellence have never been excelled.[1] A typical " Roman " of the French stage is shown us in the portrait of Molière as Cæsar (in the " Mort de Pompée ") by his friend Mignard, preserved at the Comèdie Française.

Return we now to the English stage of the Restoration. It must be remembered that pictorial art in the seventeenth as in the sixteenth century was at a low ebb. For one purely British artist then prominent we have a round dozen of foreigners. While the French stage was catered for by artists like Bérain and Lepautre, and later (c. 1752–'73) by Louis Boynet in his official capacity as *inspecteur des menus plaisirs*, and a large number of their costume-designs have been handed down to us, we have relatively scant concrete illustration of Restoration stage dress. Chappuzeau (Théâtre Français, bk. I, chap. xxiii.–a° 1674), while disposed to ridicule the English taste for thoroughness and realism in theatrical " business " says : " The English, considering their nationality [!], are quite good actors; they have very fine theatres and *splendid costumes.*" Knowing the French bias in favour of all things French, we must assume from this that Betterton's journey overseas had brought London stage-fashions into line with those of Paris. An often-reproduced but coarsely executed print of the stage at the Red Bull theatre about 1662, gives various theatrical characters in action and is of value as giving us the attire of Falstaff and Mistress Quickly; the former habited in the style of c. 1635 (there seems generally to have been an attempt to find something distinctive for this part), the latter a rather nondescript figure. Pepys' note concerning the performance of Heraclius : " the garments like Romans, very well " will not inspire much confidence in his judgment, nor is one disposed to attach much more weight to Mrs. Behn's statement (in " Oroonoko ") that the " Indian Queen's " costume at the Playhouse was one brought by the authoress from Surinam.

Nicholas Rowe's illustrated " Shakespeare " of 1709 probably affords a very fair impression of the popular notion of the appearance of the poet's characters in the next generation. As Mr. Malcolm C. Salaman aptly observes (" Shakespeare in pictorial art "; The Studio, Ltd., Spring, 1916) : " Anachronism was the rule in the matter of theatrical costume, and then, as indeed throughout the eighteenth century and as it had been in Shakespeare's own day, the actors would play any parts other than Greek or Roman [these were not differentiated], in the costumes of contemporary fashion. When an antique Roman or Greek had to be impersonated, there would be a sort of attempt to dress the part in something suggestive of

[1] See "Monumenta Scenica" (in progress), a series of albums of reproductions of designs for stage-dresses, the originals being preserved in the National Library, Vienna. Published at Vienna by the Directors of the National Library, with text in English and German.

' classic ' garb, though the actresses would rarely, if ever, condescend to
exchange their own fashionable skirts and bodices for the stola of the Roman
women or the peplum of the Greek." We might add that they also insisted
on their hair being dressed in the latest fashion, while the actors clung as
tenaciously to the full-bottomed wig. Mr. Salaman is right in drawing
attention to Rowe's illustration of " Much Ado about Nothing," but wrong
in saying : ". . . the Duke is in the mode of Charles I." " Duke " I pre-
sume to be a slip for the " Prince of Aragon "; but the figure appears to
me to be certainly " Don John," and there has been a conscientious effort
to put him into *Spanish dress*, so far as known to English folk. Except the
friar, the other figures are in full Queen Anne dress. The scene between
Hamlet, the Queen and the Ghost has a special interest, because of the
Garrick Club portrait of the great Betterton and Mrs. Barry in this very
scene, in which the characters also wear the modes of the day, the Ghost
being in a curious suit of " property " armour. The half-length portrait
of the deceased Hamlet, senior, on the wall behind presents the usual incongruous combination of armour and periwig so popular at this date. In
the scene from " Henry VIII " we have an example of a detail of tradition
adverted to elsewhere; the king and cardinal are habited and made up in
very fair imitation of the real Henry and Wolsey, the courtiers, as usual,
in full-bottomed wigs, cravats, coats and vests, etc., in the taste of the day.
The costumes and properties throughout are pretty obviously borrowed
from the stage; this is the more interesting when we recall that they are
executed in the heyday of such actors as Betterton, Wilks, Barton Booth,
Mrs. Barry and Mrs. Bracegirdle.

No special alterations, let alone improvements, appear to have been introduced into English stage-costume until far into the eighteenth century. Both
Charles II and his brother had been generous patrons of the stage in their
way; but from the accession of William and Mary for well-nigh two centuries Royalty took little intelligent interest in the stage or its productions,
nor, indeed, in the arts generally. The taste of Queen Anne, the interests
of the four Georges all lay in more material things. " Florizel " might find
in the theatre the opportunity of an intrigue with " Perdita " (George IV,
when Prince of Wales, with Mrs. Mary Robinson) or the future William
IV for a *liaison* with Dorothy Jordan; the artistic or literary appeal of the
drama left them indifferent. They were, above all, not the men, like Lud-
wig of Bavaria, to care much about the spectacular side of the thing. Pope's
well-known lines anent Booth's appearance in Addison's " Cato "—" Cato's
long wig, flowered gown and laquered chair,"—though often quoted do
not carry us very far. If Pope had (as well may have been) a sound instinct
that the setting was inappropriate, he was no very profound scholar, still
less antiquary. It was sufficient to him that he perceived an opening for
a gibe at the detested Addison, and Pope was not the man to forego it.
Addison himself has been quoted as an example of how " persons of taste
and education " took umbrage at the absurdity of the " tragic " wardrobe,

especially in " classical " subjects. Although he was assuredly a sounder scholar than his critic he, too, had no real apprehension, except as a linguist, of antiquity, and the passage in question (" Spectator," No. 42, April 18, 1711) indicates only that he objected to its cumbersome and grotesque character, not that he desired any particular historical accuracy. We learn now how armour from the Tower was lent to Cibber for " Henry V's Coronation " and as attributions to historical personages or periods were at this time ridiculously wide of the mark, Pope's line "Old Edward's armour beams on Cibber's breast " simply shows the little care for, or understanding of, certain national treasures in the eighteenth century. Addison, by the way, in another passage, implies his aversion from " a well-dressed play " as apt to detract from the credit due to a " well-written one."

But while the numerous tragedies on " classical " or exotic themes continued for a long while to be dressed after the Comédie Française pattern, Shakespeare, except for the exceptions already mentioned, continued to be dressed in the main in the fashionable taste of the day. The full-bottomed wig in particular continued to be worn here too in heroic parts even when (off the stage) it had gone out of vogue. There is a print of Quin in the part of Coriolanus (apparently a caricature). He still wears the full-bottomed, powdered mane surmounted by a ridiculous little casque topped with a huge ostrich plume; likewise the already mentioned *tonnelet* and high buskins. Howard is reported as wearing a similar wig as late as 1765 in the part of Tamberlaine.

About the middle of the eighteenth century a definite modification sets in with the reign at the Comédie Française of Voltaire, Lekain and Mlle Clairon, and this, since it reacted in a measure upon the methods of our own Garrick, deserves some slight consideration here. The French premier company had long flourished under the direct patronage of the king and court. It was no uncommon thing for the great lords and ladies to present portions of their wardrobes to the players, who hence were enabled in comedy to cut a figure worthy of the most fashionable circles. Neither by its constitution nor in the composition of its audiences was the Comédie " popular "—in the sense of democratic. Without any real or reasoned knowledge of " costume," Voltaire resented the " tragic " costume in vogue; particularly the plumed sombrero and giant peruke, traditional ever since the great Michel Baron. Without any very clear idea what he wanted—or rather, with very little notion of what accuracy required—he set his face in the direction of reform. At the Comédie Française the fashionable playwright of the day is a power. Lekain and Clairon were Voltaire's ardent disciples, and it was the latter who made the first step in the direction of greater appropriateness in costume. This she did for the first time when playing the part of Roxane in the Petit Théâtre at Versailles, if not at Bordeaux. Marmontel, her friend and erstwhile lover, says : " I went to her dressing-room, and there, for the first time, I saw her dressed as a sultana, without a hoop, bare-armed, in genuine Eastern costume." A week later she appeared as Electra in Crebillon's tragedy of that name in " the simple [?] dress of a slave, with dishevelled hair and arms loaded with chains." Shortly after she performed in another " Electra," Voltaire's version. "Henceforth," goes on Marmontel, " the players were constrained to give up the *tonnelets*, fringed gloves, voluminous periwigs and plumed hats which had so long been offensive to people of taste." [1]   We are not, however, to suppose that Mlle Clairon's innovations brought costume nearer in essentials to historic truth or character. She herself has discussed the question of costume in her Mémoirs (which often, incidentally, show her to have thought out things shrewdly enough), and is of opinion that the real antique is too " improper and mean " to be faithfully copied, being only suitable to painting and sculpture. What she did was to urge a greater concord between the character, the situation and the dress, and to do away with the absurdities and fashionable excesses of her day, notably the hoop or *paniers*. Lekain was not slow to follow suit. Having discarded the traditional trappings of tragedy, he set about designing his own dresses and, in order to pay for their execution, he was ready to make great pecuniary sacrifices. We have drawings and prints of Lekain as Abner (in "Athalie "), Achilles (" Iphigénie en Aulide "), Genghis Khan (" L'Orpheline de la Chine "), etc. In this last piece by Voltaire, the author, Lekain and Clairon made their supreme bid for " correct " spectacular setting. As a contrast with what had obtained earlier, the costumes, etc., are of interest and value; in themselves the new styles were only less incongruous than those they displaced. Do I say " displaced "? No, Marmontel's notes quoted above are too anticipatory. Despite the efforts of the author and his protagonists, years were still to pass ere the stage in general, more particularly the ladies, followed suit. Grimm says the play " L'Orpheline de la Chine " (first produced August 20, 1755) was the first occasion on which French actresses appeared without hoop-skirts; it was certainly not the last : the ladies in general, despite Clairon's example, clung more obstinately to the old conventions than the men.

Without wishing at this point to dwell further on the progress of " historical " costume on the French stage, it seems advisable, before returning to our own Georgian theatre, to mention briefly the continental tendencies towards archæological truth that became manifest in the last years of the eighteenth century. Lekain, as Achilles in Racine's "Iphigénie" had presented an involuntary caricature of the classical warrior as understood by the painter, Lebrun. In the last quarter of the century the French stage (we speak here specifically of the Comédie Française and allied semi-official companies) put on " mediæval " pieces (Leblanc de Guillet's " Albert'ᵉʳ ou Adeline," Sedaine's "Raimond V, comte de Toulouse") in which there was a definite, if uninformed, attempt to present historical plays in

[1] Cf. also the comments on Clairon's innovation in Noverre; "Lettre sur la danse et les ballets" and Arnault's "Souvenirs et regrets."

appropriate settings. The great Talma, pedantically accurate in this as in other respects, used his best endeavours to make the actor by his mere presence express the character allotted to him—with relatively successful results.

In Germany, on the other hand—a country without a dramatic literature or traditions—the worst of the old French traditions were being presented. Already in 1730 Gottsched had criticised the *mise en scène* generally accepted for each and every play in the classic repertoire, whatever the period or locale. Count Brühl and Caroline Neuber put on " historical " plays which they mounted (to the best of their limited knowledge) in the style of the period represented. Their hope, be it mentioned incidentally, was to effect a *reductio ad absurdum* of the plea for historical accuracy. The public accepted the results more favourably than had been expected. Meanwhile Lessing had been consistently damning the Germanised versions of French standard plays which were alone regarded as true, literary drama in his country. Shakespeare was the model he held up to his fellow-countrymen; Shakespeare, who was only available to them in translations of Ducis' anæmic adaptations ! Yet his efforts bore fruit in the great classical romantic school launched by Goethe and Schiller. Within the last quarter of the eighteenth century Goethe had made a hit with " Göetz von Berlichingen," " Egmont," etc., while Schiller had published " Don Carlos," " Fiesco," and " Wallenstein." The " romantic " movement of the early nineteenth century was unofficially inaugurated : the manners and customs, dress, armour, furniture, architecture, etc., of the Middle Ages and Renaissance, hitherto despised, were now assured of lip-service, if no more. This point we will have occasion to refer to casually later; it is time to see what was happening on our own stage.

As an argument against historical accuracy in Shakespeare (curiously enough it is only Shakespeare who is the bone of contention, for I have yet to meet the most modern of " high brows " who would advocate a tall, thin, bewhiskered Napoleon in " Madame Sans Gène "—a play intrinsically more obnoxious to arbitrary handling—or a " Philip the King " in " plus-fours " with a monocle) one is not infrequently told that what was good enough for Betterton, Garrick, Mrs. Siddons *e tutti quanti* should be good enough for anybody. On that line of reasoning we should resist railways, automobiles, aeroplanes and wireless. But, says the critic, the play's the thing in the last resort. Indeed ! did Cibber, or Garrick for that matter rest content with the play as bequeathed them by Shakespeare? The " happy ever after " endings invented for " Lear," " Romeo," etc., are a sufficient answer. No Yankee impresario desiring to infuse " pep " and " sob stuff " could take more liberties with his material.

But, " to return to our muttons," what in effect was being done on the English stage? Some writers tell us that the influence (such as it was) of Lekain reacted on the London stage. Garrick attempted a " character " costume and make-up for Othello; for his pains he was compared by Quin to one of the then fashionable negro-pages. Macklin attempted to portray Macbeth in Highland garb; and suggested merely a strolling piper—which brings us to the great " little Davy " and his period.

We know that in a general way Garrick and his compeers were satisfied to play Shakespeare and, in fact, " legitimate " drama in the modes of their day. It would seem that the English stage was even less concerned than the French with problems of historical accuracy. For the part of Hamlet, Garrick wore a black court suit and wig of the period (Henderson and others followed suit), as Macbeth he wore the uniform of an officer of the guards. In a Greek rôle (Agis) in 1758 he adapted—ask me not why—the habit of a contemporary Venetian gondolier. He was much praised for the realism of his "get-up "; chiefly, it seems, because he wore a close-trimmed tie (or bag)-wig, in opposition to the old-fashioned full-bottomed wig of Queen Anne's days, hitherto regarded as your only wear for tragedy. In a few parts he broke away from the current modes of the day. Thus in " Tancred and Sigismonda " he affected the garb of a Hungarian or hussar : busby, slung pelisse and frogged dolman. As Richard III he wore a costume more or less of James I's time with a furred surtout (John Philip Kemble, G. F. Cooke and Edmund Kean followed suit), while as Don John in " The Chimes " he wore a plumed hat and nondescript costume of no ascertainable period. Yet in Jeffery's " Collection of Dresses," 1757, the writer praises the stage-costume of the period as " elegant and characteristic." In 1771 Mrs. Yates played Medea in a turban and striped shawl, while Reddish, as Posthumus, wore a furred cloak and heavily laced suit. Mrs. Barry, as Rosalind, wore a furred suit and busby. In the part of Romeo, Holman wore a short jacket and knickers embellished with sewn on puffs intended to represent slashes. Mrs. Bellamy is said to have been the first English actress to discard the hoop-skirt in Dodsley's " Cleone." Fur trimmings, by the way, were held to lend a delightfully " Gothick " touch to costume. It was, in fact, in the last quarter of the eighteenth century that some attempt begins to be made at appropriate character in costume. The prevalent ignorance of " period " caused some amusing hotch-potches to be perpetrated, but at least the principle of the thing was becoming admitted. A good and diverting example of Shakespearian costume is Wheatley's painting of 1774, representing the mock-duel scene from " Twelfth Night," with Miss Young as Viola, Dodd as Sir Andrew, Love as Sir Toby, and Waldron as Fabian; no less informing is Mortimer's picture (1767) of Powell and Bensley as King John and Hubert. The new conception of costume for Shakespeare and " period " plays that was coming into vogue may be gathered roughly by reference to the unwieldy " Boydell Shakespeare " and in particular by the works of Fuseli, Smirke, Stothard, Angelica Kauffmann, Downman, Rev. Matthew Peters and others. As Max von Boehn in his excellent manual—" Das Bühnen-Kostüm "; Berlin, B. Cassirer, 1921—aptly points out, one should in these matters always allow for the contrary spirit of professional jealousy : it suffices for an actor (or still more, actress) to adopt any policy for his (or her) rival to throw himself into the opposite extreme. Thus Mlle Clairon's advocacy of more appropriate costume was balanced by Mlle Dumesnil's staunch adherence to tradition.

But with the turn of the century we are definitely approaching a clearer notion of " period " costume. We have seen that a vague feeling for something " different " was already in the air for historical or romantic plays as opposed to the eternal " modern " costume which every man could see for nothing in everyday life. There was an obscure foreshadowing of the imminent Romantic Movement. This is typified by the so-called " Spanish costume " of the French stage, and the " old German " dress exhibited on the German stage; both of them quaint mixtures of the most heterogeneous elements. But now both in literature, art and archæology a definite and critical interest is at hand. Joseph Strutt, pioneer of costume as the subject of scientific enquiry, laid the foundations of all future study by his " Regal and Ecclesiastical Antiquities," 1773; " Manners, Customs . . . of the People of England," 1774–76; " Chronicle of England," 1777–78; above all by his " Habits and Dresses," 1796–97. At the same time Grose was doing as much for military accoutrements in his "Military Antiquities,"1786–88, and " Treatise on Ancient Armour." The first writer's work was to be enlarged in scope by Planché, while in 1824 Meyrick carried Grose's work considerably further in the famous "Critical Enquiry." It was Strutt's unfinished historical novel " Queenboro' Hall " (completed by Scott and published in 1808) that apparently inspired the " Wizard of the North" to set about the "Waverley Novels." He had already fallen back on Scottish history and antiquities in his poems from 1805. The works of Scott aroused an enthusiasm and an interest in the (non-classical) past that spread over the civilised world. Dramas based on them were produced everywhere. Meantime in France the visit of Macready, Harriet Smithson and their company to Paris in 1828, gave fresh impetus to the "Romantic Movement." This had already been launched in 1827 by Victor Hugo's " Cromwell," the manifesto of the new school, followed in 1828 by " Marion de Lorme," by " Hernani " in 1830 and by " Le Roi s'amuse " in 1832. In all these the prefaces and stage-directions show an explicit preoccupation with the material features of the past. It is not necessary to refer to the great poet's novels here, any more than to the vivid romances of Dumas père. All these works betray the same spirit, which is noticeable in the latter writer's dramas of " Christine," 1827–8, " Henri III et sa Cour," 1829 and "La Tour de Nesle," 1832.

In London as early as 1823 Planché, encouraged and advised by Francis Douce and Meyrick, was designing the dresses and supervising the production for Charles Kembles' revival of " King John " at Covent Garden. From then on he was responsible for the costumes and *mise en scène* both there and elsewhere, being associated from 1831 with Mme Vestris' productions at the Olympic and subsequently at Covent Garden again. Curiously enough it was also in " King John" that Charles Kean began, in 1852, that famous series of spectacular productions in which all the resources of archæology were turned to account; artists and antiquaries of recognised standing being called in to design, advise and supervise everything concerned with dress, weapons, architecture and properties generally. Needless to say there was a certain section of the public who loudly condemned Kean—how often since have we heard this plaint?—for smothering the play beneath the accessories. Unfortunately, except in a limited number of rôles (he was a good Hamlet, a successful Mephistopheles, and a superlative Louis XI), Kean was hardly more than a sound and thoughtful actor, and as such was not always able to rise superior to his expensive trappings. From now on, however, at least in the best London theatres, there was a definite attempt to suggest the correct historic setting. But though we have seen Planché, that stickler for correct " period," in charge of Shakespearian and other productions from 1823, it was not till these ambitious *mises en scène* of the youngerKean that historical accuracy was more than theoretically conceded. A glance through Halliwell-Phillipps' edition of Shakespeare, 1851–53, illustrated by engravings of eminent actors in character, is proof enough of how little costume was understood. With scarcely an exception the dress and get-up of the actors—C. Kean himself, as Hamlet, does not escape the reproach—suggests their having been hired of a provincial costumier for some parish fête. Barry Sullivan as Hamlet with a very *décolleté* " little Lord Fauntleroy " collar, Farren as Romeo with moustache, sidewhiskers and " kindergarten " shoes, various Juliets tricked out in the style of the contemporary " Book of Beauty "—the ladies, by the way, are even worse offenders than the men—all are alike only in this : that their general " get-up " is devoid of any character whatever. Where nearly all are more or less grotesque, the costume of Hackett as Falstaff stands out conspicuous with his Vandyke lace collar, wide-cuffed Georgian coat, and *wide trousers ending in a lace frill at the ankle !* Assuredly the Garrick or Barry Jackson principle of presentation is better than these. Before leaving this part of our theme,we may quote a passage from Quincke's excellent little compendium of historic costume (" Katechismus der Kostüm Kunde "; Leipzig, 1889), as showing how late these nondescript hotchpotches lingered on the stage; the writer is himself official producer to the Leipzig civic theatre—" A single example may be quoted to show the kind of mixtum gatherum one may at any turn meet with. We allude to the costume worn by a well-known tenor (as also by many of his colleagues) when playing the part of one George Brown, an English officer, who has to relate the story of the battle of Culloden (1746). This consists of the following items : plumed slouch hat with looped-up brim of about 1650, a coat after the 1680 fashion cut shorter than ever the vogue was, long leather riding breeches with Hessian boots of c. 1800. To complete this he wears a close crop of curls *à la Titus*, also of c. 1800, with a modern moustache and imperial—it is mercy if he does not sport a full beard—ruffs and ruffles of 1530 accompanied with a *jabot* of 1780, and finally a cup-hilted Spanish rapier with hangers of 1570 [the cup-hilt does not appear, by the way, till well into the seventeenth century, but let that pass.—F.M.K.]. Not one item throughout is correct, and each belongs to a different century."

Despite these anachronisms the interest in the past with its manners and customs was steadily growing since Scott's novels had given it a fillip. In literature the historical novel (Harrison Ainsworth, G. P. R. James, etc.), in art historical *genre* painting (Maclise, Leslie, Frith) gradually became recognised schools, and tended to prepare the public for the more accurate portrayal of bygone life and manners on the stage.

In France, indeed, the influence of the romantic school was more immediately widespread. This reaction from the stilted and effete formulæ of the moribund classicists was prosecuted with a thoroughgoing vigour characteristically Latin, but alien to the more tolerant temper of our own people. Moreover, if the movement so rapidly took root and spread like flame, the ground was already prepared. Talma, perhaps the greatest of French actors, was a romantic before his time. He had been to London in his youth and seen Shakespeare played there. To his dying day he regretted that he had never been able to enact the poet's works except in Ducis' inspired travesties. He was the close friend of David, and, like him, a born revolutionary in his views. Moreover, he attached an importance hitherto unheard of to "looking the part," even where the rôle entrusted to him offered scant opportunities for acting. Thus in 1789, playing the little part of Proculus in Voltaire's " Brutus," he appeared in woollen tunic, lacerna, sandals, and bare limbs. His colleagues were scandalised,[1] but Talma doggedly persisted, and in November of the same year the actor rose at a bound to the head of his profession in M. J.Chénier's "Charles IX." For this performance he had carefully studied every available portrait, read every contemporary description of that ill-omened Valois to enable him to " live the part " more completely by the aid of costume and make-up. The result is said to have been startling, and although the Court and the die-hards disapproved, the people were delighted, and in the interval preceding the romantic movement, signs are not wanting that the hour of historic research in stage-setting is at hand.[2]

---

[1] Louise Contat burst out laughing : "Oh ! do look at Talma, doesn't he look horrid : *he's just like an antique statue !*" Mme Vestris took the innovation more to heart. "Why, Talma !" she exclaimed, "your arms are bare !"—"I wear them as the Romans did."—"But, Talma, you are wearing no breeches !"—"The Romans wore none."—*Cochon ! !*" and the lady, taking the "leading man's" hand, retired angrily.

[2] Millin ("Dictionnaire des Beaux Arts"—s.v. "Costume") gives "Charles IX" as the first production in which a consistent attempt was made to present *period*. It would seem that Vestris herself was converted from then on to Talma's notions of costume. Talma seems to have been well nigh the first to study in libraries, museums, picture-galleries, etc., and to solicit the advice of artists and antiquaries in support of the *mise en scène* of his productions ; anticipating Charles Kean, Irving, Tree, etc.

Besides those great protagonists, Hugo and Dumas, arose numerous others of the same school, such as Alfred de Vigny (" Cinq Mars," 1827; " Chatterton," 1835; " La Maréchale d'Ancre," 1835), Casimir Delavigne (" Marino Faliero," 1829; " Louis XI," 1832, " Don Juan d'Autriche," 1835, etc.), and Alfred de Musset (" Lorenzaccio," 1833). Romanticism was now well in the saddle, and its partisans demanded from the theatre the same accuracy in the setting as in treatment—at least so far as their understanding went. True it was a melodramatic, Wardour Street, accuracy akin to what has not inaptly been termed "tushery." In fact to such lengths of zeal did some enthusiasts go, that they endeavoured partly to suggest the *style Moyen Age* in everyday life. From now to the close of the Second Empire " costume " became more and more the rage. Under Napoleon III fancy dress balls were all the rage with the " smart set." A glance at " La Vie Parisienne " anywhere between 1863–70 is enough to prove the point. " Period " dresses were *the* favourite choice. Naturally this taste reacted on the stage, and costume-plays were never in greater favour. Most of Dumas' most popular novels were adapted for the theatre. Especially successful in this *genre* were Sardou's " Le Bossu " (adapted, 1863, from Feval's popular novel) and " Patrie ! " Sardou throughout his career attached considerable importance to accuracy of detail in the mounting of his historical pieces.[1]

With the middle of the nineteenth century we reach that period of elaborate production in Shakespearian and other " period " plays that culminated with Irving at the Lyceum. Realism was now the watchword. The last quarter of the nineteenth century was distinguished by a number of " costume " productions on a scale that had never hitherto been attempted. Two main influences contributed to this result; the visits of the celebrated Meiningen theatre-company and the example of Sir Henry Irving. The " Meiningen " were no less noted for their wardrobe and properties than for their excellent team-work. Their day of fame lasted from 1875 to 1890. Irving's gifts as an actor have been and are the subject of heated arguments, but even his detractors can hardly deny his consummate art and thoroughness as an all-round producer. No pains, no expense were spared to ensure perfection of detail, as much in the *mise en scène* as in the actual performance. He became his own manager at the Lyceum in 1878 and after several notable successes, began with " Much Ado about Nothing " (1882), that great series of spectacular productions with which his name will ever be associated. Particularly worthy of notice from the point of view of our present subject were the above-named revival, " Faust," " Macbeth," " The Dead Heart," " Ravenswood," " Becket " and " Henry VIII." Irving, not content with literally steeping himself

[1] Sardou's antiquarian learning was not equal to his zeal, although it would have been hard to convince him of the fact.

in the atmosphere of his subject and period, employed always the best advice and the most capable artists he could find to design dresses and properties : Seymour Lucas and Alma Tadema are examples in point— yet an obscure artist who could give him what he wanted would be as likely to satisfy him and be lavishly paid for his work; the mere name hardly counted. From now on the professional stage-designer became as indispensable as the scenic artist. Other theatres began to follow suit in due course. From the 'nineties onward any number of spectacular productions were " put on " at His Majesty's by Beerbohm Tree, and elsewhere by Sir George Alexander, Sir John Martin-Harvey, Lewis Waller, etc. Among artists particularly identified with stage costume designs are Percy Anderson, the late Percy McQuoid, the late " C. Wilhelm "[1] (W. C. J. Pitcher, *see* chapter on COSTUME IN BALLET), Herbert Norris, Tom Heselwood, to say nothing of others whose work is exemplified in the present volume.

As to whether historical accuracy in dress and *mise en scène* is desirable, I will only say this. Wherever the subject is definitely connected with an actual historical person or event, to misrepresent the outward aspects of the period referred to is definitely to mislead the ignorant spectators. In addition to the " plus-fours " version of " Hamlet," mentioned at the beginning of this paper, there have recently been performed certain scenes from the " Merchant of Venice " presented on the same principle. True neither of these plays is really a " period " play, but if they are to be presented in a 1926 setting, then why in the name of logical consistency should any of the other tragedies and comedies—I say nothing of the histories—escape like treatment, and where will that land us ? Are Romeo, Mercutio and Tybalt to roam the streets of Verona armed with swords over their lounge suits, or will they " draw " pistols in the Kentucky or Apache style? In the latter case why not transfer the scene to Dublin and make of the Capulets Republicans and of the Montagues Free Staters? But whatever we may think of Shakespeare's tragedies or comedies in modern costume, I hold that wherever a definite historic colouring or allusion (whether to persons or events) is expressly introduced into a play, it is a matter of mere probity to reproduce the atmosphere of the period as conscientiously as possible. We are told that " the stage is not an archæological lecture-room." Very true, but it has no right, out of laziness, parsimony or ignorance, to impart incorrect information to a defenceless public. The presentation on the stage or on the film of alleged historical events amounts, intentionally or not, to

His prominent association with ballets and musical comedy has obscured the fact that he was a most capable designer of "period" costumes. Indeed, he personally preferred this line of work, and showed what he could do in it by his designs for "The Armada" (Drury Lane), "Les Merveilleuses," "Tom Jones," and "Young England" (Daly's), "The Midsummer Night's Dream" and "As You Like It" (for Oscar Barrett and Robert Courtneidge's Manchester productions).

education by suggestion. As a rule, visual impressions are more vivid and durable than literary ones. If you cannot present an historical period accurately, try a different subject. There is no obligation whatever to attempt " costume " plays, still less to present them in improper guise. A man's character is even now by many gauged by his outward showing. Therefore to present an historical character in trappings unsuited to his precise period is tantamount to describing Queen Elizabeth as a shy *ingénue*, or Charles II as a Chadband.

It has often seemed to theatrical managers good policy to engage (at a high figure) the services of some fashionable painter of the day, regardless of his knowledge of history. The principle is a fallacious one : far better to retain the services of an artist of indifferent technique, but with a sound knowledge of the history of costume and fair experience of the peculiar conditions of the theatre. If he has further some knowledge of pattern and dressmaking, so much the better. He should be taken into the author's and producer's confidence : a copy of the script should be lent him to show him the " business " to which each costume must be adapted; also, he should be enlightened as far as possible as to the physical characteristics of the personnel to be clothed and made up, even down to the " chorus-gents." I remember that it was a great advantage when writing scenarios, designing costumes and casting the parts for the old Empire ballets (including "sets"—as " 4 huntsmen," " attendants on Bacchus," etc.), to have a permanent company, each member well known to the designer. I have seen on the other hand a production where the dresses were distributed among the chorus without the designer's knowledge. As a result, a costume expressly intended for a big man was given to a short light-built actor, conversely a big, burly man figured as the young Napoleon !

It has often been urged that historical accuracy is impracticable; this I deny *in toto*. I have on occasion seen on the stage figures that might almost have stepped from some mediæval or later canvas. Given knowledge, patience and a free hand, wonderful results are obtainable. Nor is mere accuracy *per se* necessarily more expensive than its opposite. A fault very characteristic of historical costume on the stage is its immaculate, fresh-from-the-tailor look, which stamps it as of the theatre, stagy. Except for wedding scenes, balls, court ceremonies and the like, every costume should be a little worn (preferably used before performance) and dulled, to give the effect of usage. Two common faults of the costumier's work are skimpiness and lack of body in the materials. Elizabethan cloaks in particular have neither the solidity nor the volume necessary to their correct " flare." There are countless details which could be mentioned whose incorrect rendering by the costumier falsifies the whole impression aimed at. Discussion of these would, however, launch us into an entirely fresh subject.

The Reinhardt school, full of the theory of "Expressionismus," and still more the latest Soviet theatres in Russia, affect a lofty contempt of realism. I have had the opportunity of seeing Moissy as Hamlet at the Grosses Schauspielhaus, Berlin. I will only say here that this performance was to me a complete novelty.

BIBLIOGRAPHY

A.—Books dealing with the Theatre and *mise en scène*.

Böhn, M. von : " Das Bühnen Kostüm " ; Berlin, 1925.*
Chappuzeau, Samuel : " Le Théâtre Français " ; (published Monval) Paris, 1875.
Clairon, Mlle : " Memoires " ; Paris, au iii.
Cunningham, P. : " Extracts from the Accounts of the Revels at Court."
Feuillerat, A. : " Office of the Revels under Queen Elizabeth " ; Leipzig, 1908.
Feuillerat, A. : " Office of the Revels under Edward VI and Mary," *ibid*, 1914.
Greg, W. W. : " Henslowe's Diary."
Greg, W. W. : " Henslowe Papers."
Jullien, Adolphe : " Histoire du Costume au Théâtre " ; Paris, 1880.
Mantzius, Karl : " History of Theatrical Art."
Monval, G. : " Costumes de la Comédie Française" ; Paris, 1884.
Nicoll, Allardyce : " History of Restoration Drama " ; 1923.
Planché, J. R. : " Cyclopædia of Costume " (vol. ii, chap. x) ; London, 1876–79.
Soulié, Endore : " Recherches sur Molière," etc. ; Paris, 1863.

* Contains an excellent bibliography of stage-costume.

(*Continued on page 32*)

BIBLIOGRAPHY—*Continued*

B.—English Books on Historic Costume.

Calthrop, D. C. : " English Costume."

Fairholt, F. W. : " Costume in England " ; London, 1885.

Hughes, Talbot : " Dress Design."

Kelly, F. M. and R. Schwabe : " Historic Costume " ; London, 1925.

Planché : *Op. cit* (*passim*).

Valuable illustrations will also be found in " Costumes of all Nations " (English edition of " Münchner Bilderbogen—Zur Geschichte des Kostüms " ; Munich, *n.d.*), and in the reproductions given in :

Böhn, M. von : " Die Mode : Menschen und Moden im Mittelalter " ; Munich, 1925.

Böhn, M. von : " Die Mode : Menschen und Moden im xvi Jahrhundert " ; *ibid*, 1923.

Böhn, M. von : " Die Mode : Menschen und Moden im xvii Jahrhundert " ; *ibid*, 1913.

Böhn, M. von : " Die Mode : Menschen und Moden im xviii Jahrhundert " ; *ibid*, 1909.

See also " Shakespeare's England " ; Oxford, 1926 (chapters by Percy McQuoid and Percy Simpson).

Böhn's books are *German*, but include illustrations of English dress.

PLATE XIV

EDWARD GORDON CRAIG
"Design for a diminutive Shakespeare Stage"

This sketch was made for a diminutive Shakespeare stage such as might be required by amateurs in distant towns in America or in the north of England where a "fit-up" is needed. The sketch (made in 1910) shows a scene which is to stand through the whole play - + is suitable for all the plays of Shakespeare. It is not difficult to build - not more difficult than usual sceneries & "fit-ups" -

It consists of a proscenium arch of about 25 feet square, with a second "arch" standing some 8 feet behind the first arch : the second arch is about 24 ft square & is raised on a step which is 2 ft high. Behind this second arch comes another step 2 feet high and about 3 to 4 feet distant from the second arch. On this step are placed two sliding walls or "doors" - which run on small wheels or rollers. Behind these are to be as many back-cloths as you need - painted to represent what you will. These back-cloths are the only parts of the scene which require painting. Your amateur group will do well to engage the services of one of the cleverer & younger members of the new movement to help carry this design further - & to light it properly. Gordon Craig.

PLATE XV

CHARLES RICKETTS, A.R.A.
" The Doge."
" Merchant of Venice."
(Y.M.C.A. War-time Productions.)

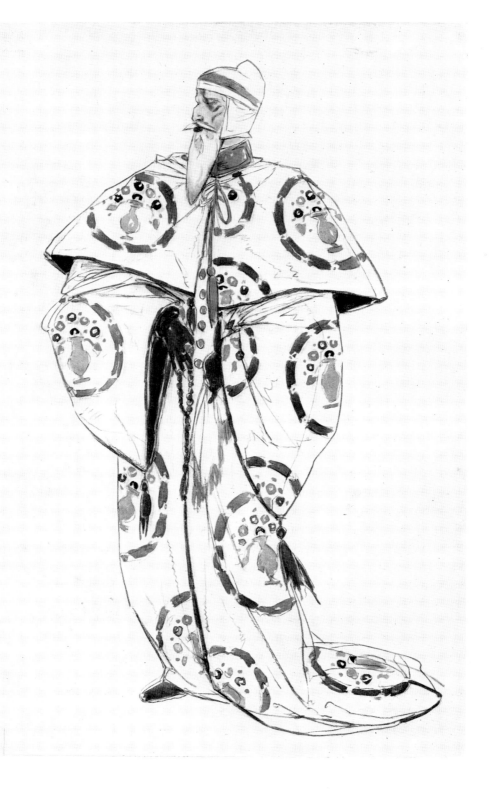

PLATE XVI

CHARLES RICKETTS, A.R.A.
" Goneril."
For " King Lear."

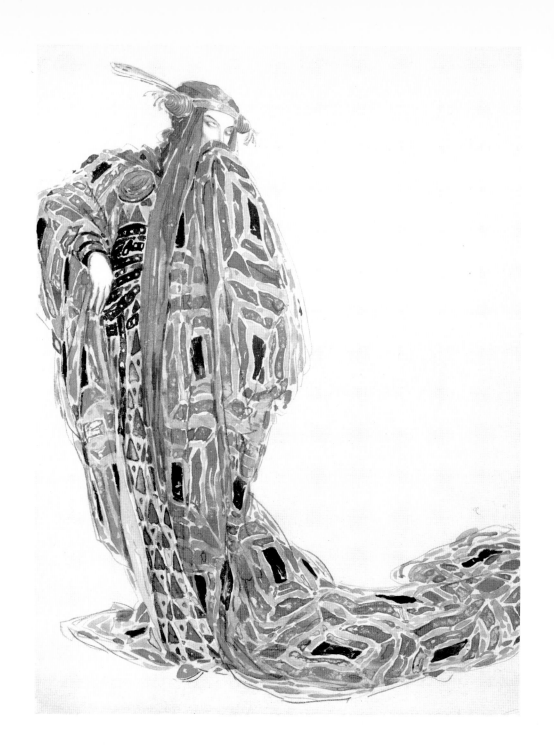

PLATE XVII

CHARLES RICKETTS, A.R.A.
"Tubal,"
"Merchant of Venice,"
(Y.M.C.A. War-time Productions.)

PLATE XVII

CHARLES RICKETTS, A.R.A.
" Tubal."
" Merchant of Venice."
(Y.M.C.A. War-time Productions.)

PLATE XVIII.

CHARLES RICKETTS, A.R.A.

"Jessica."

"Merchant of Venice."

(Y.M.C.A. War-time Productions.)

PLATE XVIII

CHARLES RICKETTS, A.R.A.
" Jessica."
" Merchant of Venice."
(Y.M.C.A. War-time Productions.)

PLATE XIX

CHARLES RICKETTS, A.R.A.
"Two Courtiers."
For " The Winter's Tale."

PLATE XX

RANDOLPH SCHWABE
" Tybalt."

PLATE XXI

RANDOLPH SCHWABE
" Costume, Henry VIII Period."

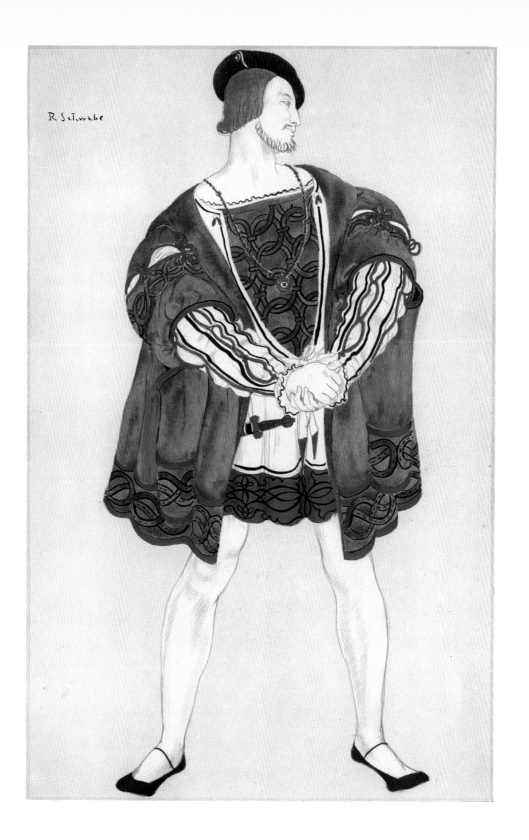

R. Schwabe

PLATE XXII

RANDOLPH SCHWABE
" Third Lady of the Court."

3rd Lady 9th Cent
Act II

PLATE XXIII

RANDOLPH SCHWABE
" Mercutio."

IX

Mercutio

R. Schwabe

PLATE XXIV

RANDOLPH SCHWABE
" Juliet."

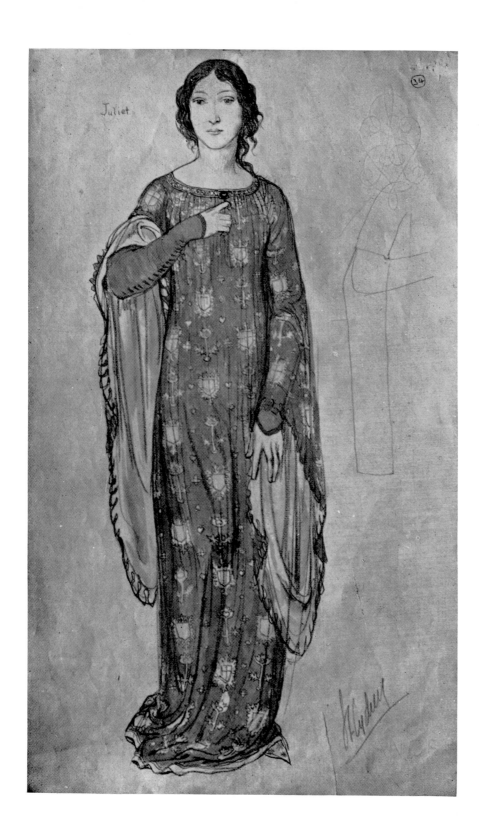

Juliet

PLATE XXV

ALBERT RUTHERSTON
" Camillo."

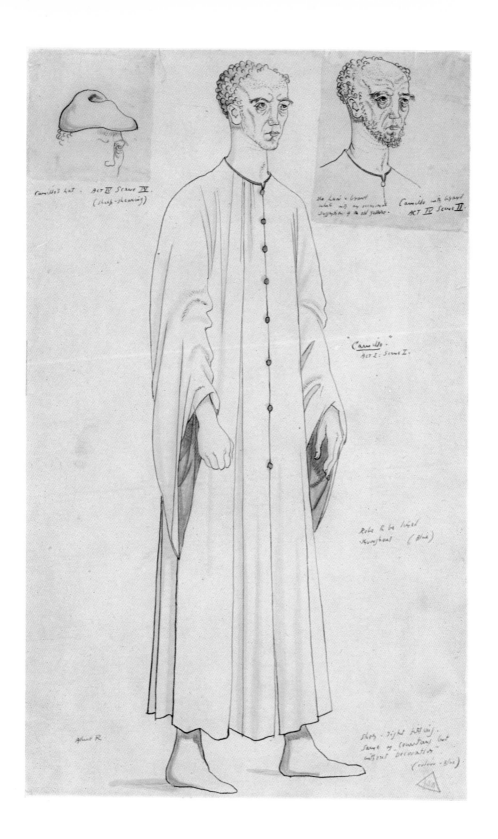

Camillo's hat . Act IV Scene IV.
(sheep-shearing)

the hair & beard
white with an occasional
suggestion of the old yellow.

Camillo with beard
ACT IV Scene II.

"Camillo"
ACT I . Scene I.

Robe to be lined
throughout . (Blue)

About R.

Shoes . tight fitting.
same as courtiers but
without decoration.
(colour . blue)

PLATE XXVI

TOM HESELWOOD
" Philip and Mary."

Philip & Mary.

PLATE XXVII

CYRIL MAHONEY
" Historic Costume."
" As You Like It."

TOM HESELWOOD
" Henry VIII and Edward VI."

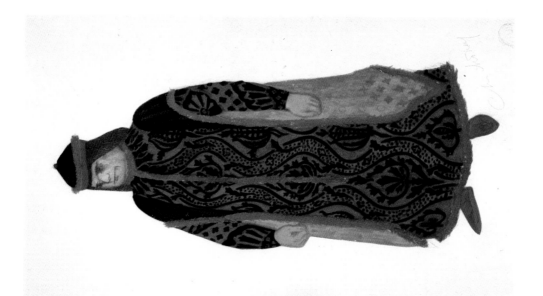

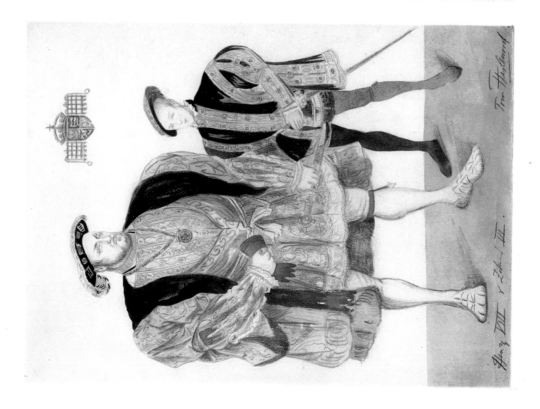

PLATE XXVIII

CYRIL MAHONEY
" Historic Costume Design."
For Zangwill's " Too Much Money."

PLATE XXIX

GLADYS SPENCER CURLING
" Spirit of the Restoration."

Gladys Spencer Curling. 1927.

PLATE XXX.

REGINALD BRILL
" Queen Elizabeth."

PLATE XXX

REGINALD BRILL
" Queen Elizabeth."

PLATE XXXI

REGINALD BRILL
" Garrick as Richard III."

PLATE XXXII

REGINALD BRILL
" Costume of 1600."

PLATE XXXIII

REGINALD BRILL

PLATE XXXIII

REGINALD BRILL
" Victorian Cleopatra."

PLATE XXXIV

REGINALD BRILL
" Hamlet."

III
IRISH DRAMATIC COSTUME

G

IRISH DRAMATIC COSTUME

By Lennox Robinson

There is a fundamental difference between the unendowed repertory theatre and the ordinary theatre, between, that is to say, a theatre which alters its programme at least every week and which repeatedly revives its plays, and a theatre at which a play is put on for as long a run as is financially possible. The difference affects every branch of the theatre's work. In the case of the ordinary theatre each play is considered as an isolated production having no relation to what may have preceded it and what may come after, players are chosen to fill but a single part, scenery is designed for use in a single play and in no other, costume is considered only in relation to one play and one player. But in a repertory theatre each production is but a link in an unending chain of plays, and the question of players, scenery and costume has got to be considered in relation to a whole season's programme— it may be in relation to a whole life's work. No new production, be it ever so successful, can immediately earn a great deal of money, it can at best but fill the theatre for a week and an elaborate production in the ordinary theatre may have to play for a month or for many months before it will have paid for its initial expenditure. Three such elaborate productions in one year would bring any repertory theatre into the bankruptcy court. Economy and compromise must be the repertory theatre's watchwords, and the aim must be not the immediate startling perfection of a single production, but the slow building-up of a company of pliable players, an accumulation of scenery that can be adapted to many plays, a wardrobe that, before everything else, is useful. Economy in the ordinary theatre is out of place, the play put on for a run must succeed immediately or altogether fail—the number of failures that have been " nursed " into successes are only exceptions for the proving of the rule—the play's campaign with the public must be a matter of brilliant attack, of dashing surprise, never a war of attrition, the ha'porth of tar must never be spared; but in the repertory theatre tar must be used as grudgingly as if it were gold-leaf.

Undoubtedly perfection of production is more quickly and easily reached when each play can be considered as an artistic entity uninfluenced by what has preceded it and taking no thought for its successor. But in the long run, and considering its work as a whole, the repertory method has been proved to give to the public a richer return, a more varied mass of plays, in the end more subtle players. I can speak with practical knowledge of only one repertory theatre—the Abbey Theatre in Dublin—with whose work I have been intimately connected these fifteen or sixteen years, and what I write now must necessarily be in relation to my experience there. That theatre has had to hasten very slowly, its fight for existence has been a protracted siege, more protracted I think than any repertory theatre's in England needs to be. We found no repertory of plays ready-made to our hand (as an English repertory theatre will find), we had to create our own playwrights, and for the last twelve years, faced as we were by three successive wars, we have been, I suppose, the poorest little theatre in the world. We could afford to risk nothing, it was only by economy of the most bitter kind that we have managed to survive.

Economy means compromise, the ceaseless practice of " making things do." Can such compromise be effected without production very grievously suffering? I think it can. In the matter of scenery—unrealistic scenery, not wall-papered interiors or cottage interiors and exteriors—we have compromised to our own satisfaction by the use of a set of screens devised a good many years ago by Mr. Gordon Craig. They are easy to handle and capable of being arranged in an endless number of combinations, in fifteen years we have not exhausted their uses, practically all our " romantic " scenes are created out of them, they are as versatile as our players.

In the matter of costume something equivalent to these screens must be sought by a repertory theatre. I do not trouble here to consider the question of costume in a modern realistic play, modern life—be the setting rich or poor—can be copied cheaply enough, though even in these plays the director of a repertory theatre should hesitate long before authorising the purchase of a hat or a coat that cannot be " made do " in at least half a dozen plays. A few modern plays may demand special costumes, in our theatre the plays of Synge that are set in the far west of Ireland make such a demand, and for them we have been at pains to copy accurately or to buy the originals of petticoat and shawl and pampootie, and in an English repertory theatre some play of primitive peasant life may need such special treatment, but generally speaking the question of costume only becomes serious—serious I mean in consideration of the circumstances which govern production in a repertory theatre—when the play to be produced is non-realistic, is "romantic." For such plays something as malleable and versatile as Mr. Gordon Craig's screens must be looked for, something than can be easily altered and interchanged. The screens are very simple in line and colour, they can hardly be made to look odd and wrong; costume is more elaborate more varied in colour, and it is very easy to go wrong.

36

But economy—compromise of some sort—is imperative and the designs of Mr. Ricketts, which illustrate this article, show how beautifully it can be achieved. They were made many years ago for our theatre, for the production of Mr. W. B. Yeats's poetical plays, for " The King's Threshold," " On Baile's Strand " and " The Green Helmet " in particular; in point of fact they have served as a stock of costumes in which any of Mr. Yeats's poetical plays can be performed. Naturally each of these plays will be likely to demand a dress or two peculiar to itself, the little princesses in " The King's Threshold," the singing women in " On Baile's Strand " are, in this sense, " peculiar "—but nearly all the other dresses are composite. Looking at Mr. Ricketts's notes on the costumes for Old, Middle-aged and Youngest King in the latter play, I see that he indicates that their caps are the pupils' caps out of " The King's Threshold," the Old King's under-dress comes from " The Green Helmet," the Middle-aged King's under-dress from " The King's Threshold " and the Youngest King wears the Chamberlain's tunic from that play. Even when Mr. Ricketts designs a costume for the hero of " The Green Helmet " he uses the same careful economy, and the dress under Cuchulain's great sea-cloak is that of the dying poet Seanchan.

But the beauty of these dresses and our theatre's poverty have made us use them for purposes that Mr. Ricketts, perhaps, never dreamed of. This large set of costumes has, in fact, furnished us with a wardrobe of beautiful stock " romantic " costumes as adaptable as Mr. Gordon Craig's screens. On their variety and richness it has been possible to draw to an almost unlimited extent. We dressed Lady Gregory's fantastic play " The Dragon " from them and the singing women's dresses which seemed to be " peculiar " to " On Baile's Strand " turned out to be perfect costumes for the little prince's fantastic aunts. Looking back over old account books I notice how in some of our poorest years we spent in three months but five pounds, eight pounds, once only 12s. 6d. on costume (and that money I am sure was spent on blouse or apron or bowler hat), yet during those years we were able to dress with distinction and beauty many a romantic play. Mr. Gordon Craig, too, once designed a set of costumes for " The Hour Glass " which we still use when we produce that play and we make as free with those dresses as we do with Mr. Ricketts's. Possibly both these artists would hold up their hands in horror could they see some of the liberties we have taken, but poverty cannot afford the higher forms of artistic punctilio.

With the passing of the years many of Mr. Ricketts's dresses have faded or worn out, and when last spring we decided to revive Mr. Yeats's "Deirdre" and had a little money to spare, we asked a young Irish artist, Miss McGuinness, to design a set of costumes for it. It is very interesting to compare her designs with Mr. Ricketts's, they are the antithesis of the " stock " costume, they are designed definitely for a certain play which is to be played in a scene of such and such a colour, they are, that is to say, more in the tradition of a play that is to be put on for a run than in the tradition of a repertory theatre. In the case of a revival of " The King's Threshold " or of " On Baile's Strand," we are bound in no way to stage the play in the scene in which it was staged before; always a little dissatisfied with ourselves we will probably try a new arrangement of the screens, splash them perhaps with a different colour, and by some miracle Mr. Ricketts's dresses will compose themselves into the scene, will always look noble and beautiful. Miss McGuinness's dresses are no less effective and beautiful, but they belong very definitely to a single play and a single setting, Mr. Ricketts's costumes can be used with others of plain dyed hessian and no false note is struck, but only Miss McGuinness can add a costume to Miss McGuinness. They have not the rich abundance of the older dresses, one could not take a cloak from one, an ornament from another, a head-dress from a third and, combining them with other odds and ends, build up a new costume. Mr. Ricketts's costumes have been our very humble servants, Miss McGuinness's will probably loll in idleness in a wardrobe until " Deirdre " is produced again.

It seems a little ungracious to compare these artists' work to the disparagement of the younger's, when I and many others have got so much delight from Miss McGuinness's designs, but the contrast between them illustrates the point I wish to make. The repertory theatre's costume must be a compromise, it must deal in generalities rather than in peculiarities. This does not mean that it need be shabby or dull, but that, perhaps, its general tone must be a little low. The lowest note can be fittingly and beautifully struck by very plainly-made dresses of hessian dyed in some rich colour or plainly grey, they should be without embroidery or ornament, they are to be worn by soldier and serf and peasant. Against their simplicity a beautiful dress on King or Queen or Princess will stand out in sharp contrast.

But if the idea of the composite dress is shocking, if it smacks too much of the rag-bag, of children " dressing-up " to while away a wet afternoon, there is an alternative course. Is there any reason why a costume should not move unaltered from play to play? A repertory theatre might start for itself a beautiful convention of costume, and a Shakespearian theatre be at pains to create a splendid costume for its King, a costume that Lear would wear in his first act, and Richard III. in his fourth act, and Claudius throughout "Hamlet." Add to it a costume for a queen, a prince, a princess, a fool and half the Shakespearian wardrobe is complete and there is no harm, there is much to be said, for the audience recognising the character from the costume, nudging itself and whispering " Here comes the King." A repertory theatre having such a convention might find some rich patron who would present it with a queen's dress, some wealthy idle lady, perhaps, who would stitch the dress with her own fingers, or the theatre's gallery might put their sixpences together and gather enough to buy a beautiful costume for a fool and the dress might become as recognised and loved as the face of any favourite player.

It is becoming the fashion among producers to think of a play only in its supreme moments and to plan scenery and costume in relation to those moments, to strive for one or two startling symbolical effects. The producer in a theatre where costume and scenery must be " made do " will seldom be able to afford such effects, he will have to remain in the older fashion and think of a play as a series of moments each one emotionally different from the other, a series of pictures. He will, therefore, require material which is not too definitely stamped with any one emotion, scenery very simple and of some plain flat colour—Mr. Gordon Craig's screens or some arrangement of curtains, costume, unobtrusive in the mass but with some sharp contrast in colour, in richness, in elaboration—Mr. Ricketts's beautiful cloaks or a conventionalised Shakespearian king. This older fashion seems to me more artistically true than the other, and I do not regret that the theatre I work in, being poor and a repertory, forces me to adhere to it.

IRISH COSTUME AND THE THEATRE

By Gerald Macnamara

With illustrations by the Author

Until the Irish National Theatre and the Ulster Literary Theatre came into being, at the beginning of this century, the general public in either Great Britain or Ireland knew little or nothing about the costumes of the old Irish, with the exception, perhaps, of the designs from the Book of Kells and what is known as the " Tara " brooch. Indeed, until that time the Irish public knew more about the costumes and the manners of the Romans of the first Cæsar's age than they did about those of their own national heroes. There was, however, some excuse for them, for knowledge lay mostly hidden away in inaccessible libraries, and it was the knowledge, moreover, of archæologists and dry fellows generally. Books on ancient Ireland were hardly ever illustrated, except with engravings of ruined Round Towers and the sites of mythological battles. Even Irish artists left the dark ages of their native history untouched, a history with a mythology rivalling that of Greece, certainly better than anything in the Niebelung Lied.

That movement which has been for convenience' sake, though incorrectly, described as the Irish Literary Renaissance—the Gaelic League, and, later, the Irish National Theatre, of Dublin, and the Ulster Literary Theatre (now the Ulster Theatre), of Belfast—opened up a new vista to those interested in Ireland. Ancient Ireland came out of the nebula of Romance, where harps, Round Towers, lean wolf-hounds, Tara Halls and Scriptures, and brooches seemed inextricably mixed up in the manner of the native intaglio ornament. Even the shillelagh and the be-ribboned bog-oak pipe were thrown overboard as emblems of Ireland's independence. The incomparable beauty of ancient Irish design, ornament, and costume had been re-discovered.

The ancient Gaels possessed the tribal system and for this reason were a fighting people. We may take it for granted, therefore, that their garments were warlike but simple. From the descriptions of costumes in the Bardic literature one would come to the conclusion that the ancient Irish and the ancient Greek costumes had many points of resemblance. Both peoples wore a short-sleeved tunic and a cloak, but it is natural to assume that the Irish garments were of a much heavier material. With the Irish the tunic was often striped or chequered in bright colours.

THE TUNIC

H

41

In the extremely early eras, the manners and ceremony of the tribal courts were naturally rude and uncouth, very different from the pomp and circumstance that attended the court in Tara in later days when one king, the Ard-Ri, ruled all Ireland. These minor kings wore a crown of gold, but wore it only on the battle-field as a guide to their followers, and, incidently, to their enemies. The kings of those dark days, even in the later times of Tara, only held their position by virtue of their prowess in battle. The " Divine Right " was as yet unheard of. On state occasions they dressed themselves in costly robes, the better to impress their subjects, and the emissaries of tributary princes.   Let us take an old chronicler's description of King Cormac Mac Art on one of these state occasions :

" His hair was slightly curled, and of a gold colour. A scarlet shield, with engraved devices and having golden loops and clasps of silver. A wide-flowing purple mantle around him. A gem-set gold brooch on his breast. A gold torque around his neck. A white-collared robe, embroidered with gold upon him. A girdle with golden clasps and studded with precious stones around his waist. Two shoes of gold net-work, with golden buckles. Two spears with golden sockets and many red bronze rivets in his hand, while he stood in the manly glow of beauty, without defect or blemish."

The kings of ancient Ireland, like the chieftains and other fighting men, do not seem to have worn beards. It is evident that only scholarly men, such as the Brehons (the law-givers), the Shenachies (the historians), the bards and the minstrels were bearded. In that enthusiastic chronicler's description of Cormac there are one or two touches that seem worthy of further examination by the designer of theatrical costumes. The " scarlet shield," for instance, suggests something infinitely more decorative than the conventional one of bronze. Variously coloured shields with engraved bosses would have a very striking effect on the stage. A " wide-flowing purple mantle " indicates a very large mantle, reaching at least from head to heel. The purple, however, is not essential, as in those days kings, we are told, dressed in crimson and other brightly coloured mantles as well.

There are many designs af ancient Irish brooches, but the " Tara " design is so characteristically Irish that it should be selected in preference to any other. The " Torque " is a collar of twisted metal, either silver or gold, and was a symbol of royalty, the same as the crown. The artist will have an opportuniy in the " white-collared robe" of displaying his skill in designing Celtic ornament in the gold embroidery, which should run down the front and round the hem of the robe. The girdles, buckles, shoes, etc., I shall describe later on.

As for the Irish chieftain, he was usually at war, and dressed in a costume that gave him as much freedom of movement as possible. His hair was long, but not so long as Absalom's. It touched his shoulder and,

THE "TORQUE"

according to the ancient chronicles, was almost invariably "yellow." (The word "golden" is only used in referring to ladies or to kings.) It was cut short in the front, with the exception of one long tuft known as the " glib." In later years the " glib " was a great source of annoyance to the early British settlers of Tudor times. English settlers were forbidden to dress their hair after that fashion, as it seemed to the authorities, to make them " more Irish than the Irish themselves." The Gaelic chieftain wore a fillet round his head. It might be of any material—gold, silver, copper, bronze, leather, or cloth. It could be adorned, sometimes, with jewels. For theatrical purposes, the fillet is not only decorative, but useful in keeping the wig in position. Helmets we rarely find mentioned, so rarely indeed, that I imagine they must have been merely *spolia opima* from invaders, probably Norsemen. The chieftain wore a tunic with short white sleeves. It was a very roomy affair, reached to the knee, and was open at the neck. Usually it was made of wool, and as the ancient Irish were skilled in the use of dyes, their tunics were to be seen dyed brightly in all colours, sometimes striped, sometimes chequered, though saffron seems to have been a favourite shade. Tunics were also made of leather, studded with bronze plates or pieces

THE FILLET

of horn sown with the sinews of animals. The purpose, I fancy, was armorial in the practical sense rather than in the decorative. Silken tunics were also worn, though hardly in action, and for the winter months there were hooded tunics, something like those worn by the English mediæval villein. The tunic lends itself to the art of the embroiderer, with bands round the sleeve, on the edge of the skirt, down the body, or in detached design all over the garment.

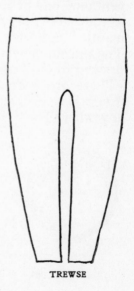

TREWSE

SHOE

As a rule, the chieftain wore nothing from the knees downward, except shoes and the straps attached to these, which were wound either round his ankles, in the manner of the footballer of to-day, or cross-gartered, like Malvolio. Trewse, of course, were commonly worn. These were like "peg-top" trousers, but saved from this awful appearance by the shoe

43

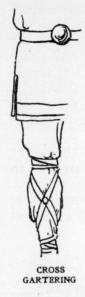

CROSS
GARTERING

straps being crossed in a trellis pattern up to the knee. The kilt also was worn, but many of the annalists describe it as an apron reaching to a little above the knee. As the kilt was often of leather, it was hardly possible to pleat it like the Scottish kilt.

The mantle was a very important garment to the Irish warrior. It made him look dashing by day; by night it was often his bed and bedding. It was either a perfect square or, like the Roman toga, a perfect circle with a hole cut out in the centre and a slit made from this to the hem. The warrior glorified his mantle as he did his sword and shield and decorated it accordingly. The mantle was, like the tunic, dyed in the most striking of colours, sometimes several shades on one garment, and decorated with designs worked in appliqué, and usually of cloth. Cloaks worn on feast days were embroidered with gold and silver threads.

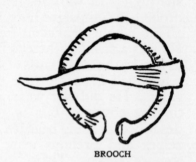

BROOCH

Shoes were the only form of footwear. According to the chroniclers, they were of many patterns and of different kinds of skins. Among the chieftains, they were of fine tanned leather, covering the toes and part of the instep, in some cases exposing the whole upper part of the foot. For fighting men "in action," the producer might employ goatskin moccasins.

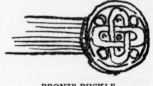

BRONZE BUCKLE

The ancient Irish chieftain wore almost as many accoutrements in battle as the Roman legionary. Belts, straps and girdles heavily studded with rivets are constantly being alluded to. The rivets, especially, give a very decorative effect to the leather gear, being made of copper, brass, and sometimes of gold, and silver.

In regard to weapons, the chieftain used a short sword, like the Roman sword. It was much wider in the middle than at the hilt and was double-edged. The hilt was often made of ivory, richly carved, sometimes gold or silver, sometimes made of bronze, but always, according to records, ornamented. The scabbard was also an object of the craftsman's skill. On the battlefield, the warrior had his sword slung on his back with the hilt above the shoulder. It had to be out of his way, for first of all he had to attack his enemies with stones, darts, and spears. The ancient Irish were, as may be imagined, infantry in every sense of the word. Spear heads were broad, with a light, but strong shaft and a large ferrule. Loose metal rings, we are told, " ran along the shaft and made music." The shield was a very important part of the equipment. It was generally circular in shape and slightly convex. In the centre of it there was usually a large boss, ornamented, but made to carry ammunition—usually a large stone. The shield had sharp edges of exquisite fretwork, beautiful to look upon, but painful to touch. The stage designer will find many opportunities for ornament in the shield, which was often of bronze, sometimes of leather, but always decorated, at least, those of the chieftains. Hammers were occasionally employed as weapons.

Chariots were little used until the Christian era, and even then very sparingly. In warfare, tents were employed to house the troops, but in prolonged campaigns huts, made of wood and mud, were erected.

Throughout all ancient Ireland, the bard was a man of great consequence. He was a scholar, the chieftain was not, and his knowledge was imparted to him by the older bards who themselves had been given it by their elders. He did not wear any distinctive costume, but is generally described as being bearded. Shenachies and Brehons wore flowing sombre robes. They, too, were bearded. The Brehons carried a branch of a tree, hung with little bells to preserve order at their gatherings. This was known as the "craveceol." The druid priests were attired in white flowing robes and, at ceremonies, wore a crown of oak leaves.

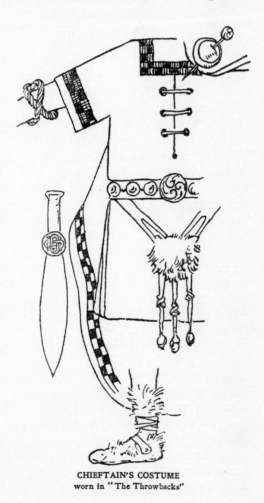

CHIEFTAIN'S COSTUME
worn in "The Throwbacks"

The noble women of Ireland were extremely gorgeously dressed. They wore their hair in a variety of fashions, sometimes streaming down with a fillet of gold across the brow, sometimes made "into three tresses, two tresses round her head and a tress behind, so that it struck her thighs behind her." Sometimes she wore it in two tresses hanging down below the waist over the breast and clasped with rings of gold. In no case was the hair short. Fillets, which were worn over the ears, were worked in precious stones and metals. The women wore shoes

LADY'S COSTUME
worn in "Thompson in Tír-na-n'-Óg"

which covered their toes and which had buckles of bright jewellery. For an impression of this costume I would refer you to the drawings of the dresses worn in " Thompson in Tír-na-n'-Óg " and "The Throwbacks."

Let us consider, now, the practical side of designing and making Irish costumes for the stage. It is really a very simple matter and does not require any great sartorial ability. The cheapest and best material for the men's costume is white flannelette, dyed. If the amateur dyes his cloth, he will be certain to get beautiful effects of broken colour (through bad workmanship, of course !) which it would be impossible to get from a web bought in a shop. Even better results can be got by dyeing the material twice. For instance, if saffron is required, dye first with pale yellow and then with bright red. Leather effects for leg straps, girdles, etc., may be had by using tan-dyed felt cloth, the kind that is used by upholsterers. Shoes can also be made from this material which is easily cut out and easily sewn.

Bands of colour or ornament can be either stencilled or sewn on the tunic or mantle. If a quiet effect is wanted, stencilling will do, but if one wants a bright red band on a blue cloth, for instance, the work should be appliqué —that is to say, one cloth cut out and sewn on to the other. This, of course, is troublesome, but purity of colour cannot be got by stencilling alone.

Women's costumes should be of a much finer material, such as mercerised lawn and velveteen. Broad girdles and fillets can be made effective with clusters of imitation pearls and beads. Bracelets and armlets can be made from flattened lead piping of different bore, painted with gold or aluminium paint.

The Ulster Literary Theatre, or Ulster Theatre, as it is now called, has done more than a little to give the public an idea of the dress and manners of the ancient Irish. It has, no doubt, specialised to a large extent in modern folk plays, but during its existence has produced no fewer than eight plays, written by Belfast authors, with scenes laid in the older Ireland. The first, produced twenty years ago, was Mr. Bulmer Hobson's "Brian of Banba." The following year was staged "The Little Cowherd of Slainge," by Mr. Joseph Campbell. The very beautiful costumes in these plays were designed by Mr. John P. Campbell, brother of the author, who has recently distinguished himself in New York with his stage decorations for the Moscow Art Theatre of Stanislawsky, and were made by the women members of the company. Some years later came Lewis Purcell's "The Pagan," with its scene laid in the dun of an Irish chieftain in early Christian times. In 1911 was produced my fantasy, "Thompson in Tír-na-n'-Óg," which I wrote with the object of making the Belfast people take an interest in the history of ancient Ireland, I might almost say,

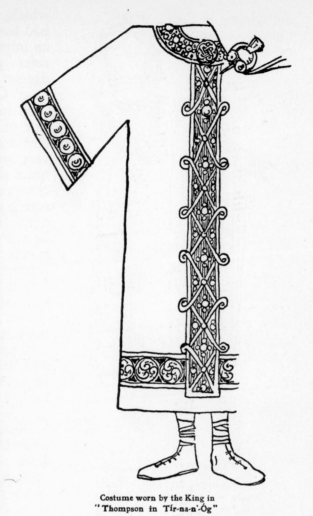

Costume worn by the King in
"Thompson in Tír-na-n'-Óg"

whether they liked it or not. This was done by introducing a North of Ireland Orangeman among the heroes in the heaven of the ancient Irish. I followed this play up a few years after with "The Throwbacks," the middle act of which takes place outside the palace gates of Tara, and then with "Fee Faw Fum," in which the costumes were a fantastic mixture of ancient Irish and modern Irish, English, and Scotch. The latest costume play to be produced by the Ulster Theatre is Mr. Rutherford Mayne's "Phantoms," dealing with Ireland in the Bronze Age. The production received great praise from no less an authority than Mr. W. B. Yeats.

The Irish theatre has passed through stormy days, and none stormier than during the last years of what we all, of no matter what denomination, refer to as "The Troubles." Brighter days seem to have broken for us, and with the wealth of Celtic design and the lovely grace of the ancient Irish costume as our resources we still hope to work small, but no less important, miracles of stagecraft.

Costume worn by Angus in "Thompson in Tír-na-n'-Óg".

COSTUME OF THE ANCIENT IRISH BARDS AND HARPERS

By Samuel Leighton

With illustrations by the Author

" In no country in Europe, is the antiquity and influence of the harp thrown so far back into the darker regions of history as in Erin. Our traditions are more distinct than those of the Greeks ; for they give time and place, name and occasion. Ours is not the shadowy myth of Orpheus going to the realms of Pluto, and by his lyre softening the obdurate heart of the grim monarch of the infernal abodes. It possesses something much more of real life, and belongs more to definite history, and from the very remotest period to which our oldest traditions refer, we find music, musical instruments, musical performers, and the power and influence of music spoken of."
O'Curry's "Manners and Customs of the Ancient Irish." (Vol. III, p. 212).

That art played an important part in the public and private lives of the ancient peoples of the world, long before the Christian era, we have ample and undoubted evidence in both sacred and secular writings of the period.

Its influence upon the emotional nature has been very marked, whether in joy or grief; amid the pastoral scenes of the shepherd's life, or the roar and clangour of battle; in celebrating the visitor's return, or honouring the departing guest; in the merriment of the feast, or the mourning of the death chamber; in all phases of life, music has ever held an important place.

The desire to express the emotions of our human nature in musical sounds has been implanted in our breasts from the earliest times. The first whisperings were doubtless very simple, imperfect and crude, but as our intellectual faculties developed, the simple sounds gradually assumed form and became more varied, and thus from the simple notes of Jubal on his lyre, or the mechanical beat of the rude savage on his primitive drum, we pass through all the transitional stages up to the magnificent orchestration of the present time, and from the monotonous chant of the ancients, to the sublime inspirations of Bach, Handel, Wagner and Elgar.

The origin of stringed instruments was probably first suggested by the twang of the hunter's bow-string, and he who first conceived the idea of affixing a second string with a different pitch, started a principle which was destined to be the beginning of the evolution of the great family of stringed instruments of music.

Antiquaries have laboured with great assiduity to reveal to us something of the past history of music, and to a large extent, have succeeded, for, explorations amongst the ancient tombs of Egypt and elsewhere have proved beyond dispute, that the art of music was known and practised from 5,000 to 6,000 years ago. We find the lyre, harp and other instruments not only painted in fresco on the walls of the tombs of great personages who lived

I   49

thousands of years ago, but we have samples of the actual instruments which were buried with the mummies, and have lain there in the darkness and silence of the tomb throughout the ages.

Ancient Greece was famous for its skill in music; the great god Pan made music upon the reeds drawn from the river, and the Apollo lyre was the nursling of the Greeks, never absent from Greek life.

" Great Apollo, let his divinity overflowing,
    die in music, through the vales of Thessaly."

The graceful lyre formed from the tortoise shell, is attributed to Hermes, and is the typical form to this day. There are various mythological legends as to the origin of the tortoise-shell lyre. The following is given in Dr. Burney's " History of Music " :—

" The invention of the lyre is attributed to the Egyptian god, Hermes, or Thoth. Hermes walking along the banks of the Nile, happened to strike his foot against the shell of a dried tortoise, and was so pleased with the sound it produced, that it suggested to him the first idea of a lyre, which he afterwards constructed in the form of a tortoise and strung it with the dried sinews of dead animals."

THE TORTOISE LYRE

From the East the movement of the ancient nations flowed Westward, the utmost geographical limit being the Isle of Erin, which has been associated with the harp from a very early age. The most ancient representation of a sculptured harp in Erin is to be found in the old church of Ullard, County Kilkenny, and dates from about the year A.D. 800 ; it is said to be the "first specimen of the type without the front pillar which has been found out of Egypt."

THE "ULLARD" HARP
From Bunting's " Ancient Irish Music "

The figure is taken from one of the ornamented compartments of a cross, carved in the usual Irish style. The stone is very much weather-worn and indistinct.

The old Irish bards were held in great respect and ranked very high in social life even at the Court of the Kings. There were several orders of bards, the Ollave being in the foremost place. They were very learned men, and only admitted to the position after twelve long years' preparation and study. The course included poetry, law, history, and story-telling. The harpers were of an inferior class, but it is not unreasonable to assume that some of the Ollaves might have been musicians as well as poets.

The following short ancient poem which Dr. Keating quotes from the " Saltair of Cashel," written about 900 A.D., but compiled from older books, refers to the two classes of poets and harpers :—

" The two renowned sons of Milesius,
Who conquered both Erin and Albain;
With them hither there came
A comely poet and a gifted harper,
Cir, the son of *Cis*, was the fair haired poet;
The harper's name was Ona the fair haired;
For the sons of the noble renowned Milesius
Was the harper wont to tune his harp."

The term " bard " seems to have been used in reference to both poets and musicians, but there was a clear distinction between the two orders. The harper, although of an honourable and numerous class, was distinct from the bard or filé, who was a verse maker, historian and reciter of tales. In later times the two became associated under the one term, and " bard " became suggestive of the harper only.

Carolan, who was born in 1670 and died in 1738, was called " the last of the bards." A beautiful bas-relief portrait has been erected to his memory in St. Patrick's Cathedral, Dublin.

About one thousand years B.C., during the reign of Tigearnmass, there is a notice of ancient law relating to the dresses to be worn by different ranks of people, whereby they were personally distinguished.

Servants were entitled to wear one colour only, husbandmen two, warriors and soldiers three, gentlemen four, chiefs five, ollaves or chief poets six, and the king and queen were distinguished by having seven colours in their dress; it is from this custom, as we read in the Book of Leinster, " that all those colours have come into the vestments of a bishop at this day."

An old Irish MS. gives us some insight into the clothing of the ancient harper :—

" I saw nine others with nine bushy curling heads of hair, with nine light blue floating cloaks upon them, and nine brooches of gold in them, nine crystal rings upon their hands; a thumb-ring of gold upon the thumb of each of them; ear clasps of gold upon the ears of each; a torque of silver around the necks of each; nine shields with golden emblazonments over them on the wall. Nine wands of white silver were in their hands. ' I knew them,' said he; ' they were the king's nine harpers.'" O'CURRY, (Vol. III, p. 146).

Vallancy tell us " that the bards wore a white mantle and a blue cap ornamented with a gold crescent."

According to McCurtin, " the Irish bards, in the sixth century, wore long flowing garments fringed and ornamented with needlework, and as many of the bards were of high degree, their dress, in some respects, would probably be similar to the nobles of the court."

" From the evidence of a bas-relief found in the ruins of New Abbey, near Kilcullen, County Kildare, it appears that the dress of the bards consisted of the truise, long cotaigh and cochal, and barréd (conical cap).

AN IRISH BARD
From Walker's "Irish Bards"

1. The *truise* or *bracca* was a tight fitting hose, covering the whole feet, legs and thighs, striped with colours according to the rank. It is from this word (*truise*) we get the Scottish ' trews,' or ' trousers.'

2. The long *cota*, or *cotaigh,* was a kind of skirt made of plaided stuff, or linen, dyed yellow, ornamented with needlework. It was open in front and extended half way down the thigh and fastened with a girdle round the waist. The sleeves came down to the wrists and turned up with a kind of military cuff, or were cut off above the elbow.

3. The *cochal* was the upper garment, a kind of long cloak, reaching down to the ankles and fringed with borders like shagged hair. From the neck at back and shoulders, was a large cape or hood ornamented with curious needlework. The beard was long and the hair fell back over the neck and shoulders."   J. C. WALKER's " Irish Bards," 1786.

The dress of the Irish bards cannot very well be authenticated, and it is only by descriptions culled from the ancient MSS., sculptures, missals, etc., that we can gain any information likely to be correct.

The accompanying illustration is taken from an early illuminated MS. of G. Cambrensis, copied from Planché's " National Costume." The date is about the thirteenth century. The hair is long and held with a golden fillet, and the harper wears the long outward garment, similar to that already described.

The barréd was a conical cap which the ollave was entitled to wear, when he was qualified for office.

An ancient writing (about B.C. 100) describes the dress of the king's poets :—

" ' I saw three others there,' said Ingcel, ' with three bands (blades or crescents) of gold across their heads; (they wore) three speckled cloaks upon them; and three shirts with red interweaving (of gold). They had three brooches of gold in their cloaks, three wooden spears (hung) over them at the wall.' ' I know them,' said Fer Rogain, 'they are the king's poets, Sin, Ro Sin, and For Sin (that is sage, great sage and greater sage).' " O'CURRY (Vol. III, p. 139).

IRISH HARPER
From an Ancient Missal

In the year A.D. 192, a code of sumptuary laws was enacted, from which we learn something of the value of the clothes of the poets and bards.

" ' The lawful price of the clothing of an ollave, or poet laureate, and of the anra, or second poet, is five milch cows.' Three milch cows is the value of a free poet's clothing, and of his wife's; it is the same from the chief bard of a flaith (petty prince) to the ollave, or poet laureate."

J. C. WALKER's " Irish Bards," p. 30.

" In the diary kept in Ireland in 1599 by Henry Harvey, sometime secretary to Robert Devereux, Earl of Essex, there is a very graphic description of an Irish harper, 'who was in truth a man very old and venerable to look on, having a long white beard which fell to his breast. His clothes were of green flannel made after his country's manner, belted in at the waist and falling below the knee; his legs bare, only for short hose of wool, and his feet shod with shoes or buskins of wolf-skin, the hair outside, tied with two thongs across the instep, the toes and heels flat, and the name of them *pampooties* or *pampooters*.' His head also was bare, the hair on it of a snowy whiteness falling heavily over the forehead in a *glibber*." " Ulster Journal of Archæology," July, 1906.

The Druids, uniformly dressed in a long, white robe emblematical of innocence and purity, and the flowing beard was as familiar as the fillet of oak leaves—perhaps the ollave copied them to some extent, but Dr. Douglas Hyde says " The popular conception of the bard with the long white beard and the big harp is grotesquely wrong."

The description of the Irish dress of the people, by Giraldus Cambrensis, bishop of St. David's in Wales, and secretary to King Henry II, who visited Ireland in the twelfth century, perfectly corresponds with that of the Belgic Gauls and Southern Britons, of the period.

" The Irish retained their ancient arms and clothing for centuries after England became a Roman province and adopted the costumes of their conquerors. The *truise*, or *braccha*, the *cota* and mantle fastened by a brooch or bodkin on the breast or shoulder, the torques, bracelets of gold and silver, swords, battle-axes of mixed copper and tin, spears and darts, headed with the same metal, had gradually superseded the garments of skins and the weapons of bone and flint of the original colonists, and were adopted as the habits and arms of the Irish chieftains during the early ages of Christianity, and to the period at which the authentic history of Ireland commences."   Planché's " National Costume of Ireland."

There is a great deal of glamour associated with the bardic period of Irish history, but, much that is really tangible, has been made known to us by the devoted labours of Professor E. O'Curry, M.R.I.A., Dr. P. W. Joyce, M.R.I.A., Dr. Geo. Petrie, R.H.A., and others, who have given earnest research amongst the records of the ancient Irish MSS.

Meantime, leaving the mists and obscurities of tradition and emerging into the clearer light of modern history, we are fortunate in being able to describe with certainty, the dress and personal appearance of some of the harpers of two hundred years ago.

Towards the end of the eighteenth century, well meaning efforts were made to rescue the harp music of Ireland from oblivion.

One of the last attempts was the celebrated meeting of harpers at Belfast in July, 1792, at which ten harpers presented themselves for the purpose of having the melodies which they were in the habit of playing, recorded in permanent form, by being transcribed into musical notation. Mr. Bunting was engaged to do this work, which he entered upon with great enthusiasm.

Six of the ten were blind, amongst them being Denis O'Hampsay, who lost his sight at three years of age. He achieved both name and fame, partly on account of his skill as a harpist and

DENIS O'HAMPSAY
1695-1807

54

partly because of the great age to which he lived (112 years). Bunting was greatly interested in him and tells us : " that he was the only one who literally played with crooked finger nails, with which he plucked the strings, closely following the action of the quills as in the old spinet. He caught the string between the flesh and the nail, not like the other harpers of his day, who pulled it by the fleshy part of the finger only."

He was the only one who played the very old aboriginal music of the country, and this he did in a style of such finished excellence as persuaded the editor (Bunting) that the praises of the old Irish harp in Cambrensis, Fuller, and others, were no more than a just tribute to that admirable instrument and its then professors." He spent many years travelling through Ireland and Scotland, and was held in great repute. He had the distinction when in Edinburgh in 1745, to play before Bonnie Prince Charlie, and sang the first tune called for :—   " I hope to see the day

> When the whigs shall run away,
> And the king enjoy his own again."

It was O'Hampsay to whom Goldsmith referred in his essay on the " Last of the Bards."

Rev. Sir H. Harvey Bruce was a good friend and looked personally after his comfort in his old age. "The day before he died, when this gentleman called upon him, O'Hampsay desired to be raised in bed and his harp given to him. After striking a few notes of a favourite melody, he was unable to proceed, and thus took his farewell to his beloved harp which had been his joy and his companion through his prolonged life of 112 years."

The Rev. Geo. Sampson, of Londonderry, wrote an appreciation of O'Hampsay, of which this is a short extract.

His dress was typical of the period; the knee-breeches, long woollen stockings, low heeled shoes with broad buckles, long tail coat and the quaint three-cornered hat, supply us with a perfect picture of the last of a famous line of Irish harpers, the expression on his venerable face, as he intently listens to the music of his beloved harp, has been well caught by the artist.

His harp is preserved in Sir H. Bruce's home at Downhill, Co. Derry, and bears the following inscription :—

> " In the days of Noah I was green,
> After the flood I've not been seen;
> Until seventeen hundred and two, I was found
> By Cormac Kelly, underground;
> He raised me up to that degree,
> Queen of music, they call me."

Patrick Quinn was the youngest of those who attended the Belfast Festival, and afterwards became instructor to the " Irish Harp Society," Dublin. Bunting remarks that he was the only one who attempted " St. Patrick's Day," of which he was very proud. He was selected to play at a commemoration to Carolan in the Rotunda, Dublin, in 1809, and was patronised by Mr. Bernard Trotter, who engaged him to play to his guests at his home in Clontarf, where he was placed in an arbour in the grounds in which picturesque surroundings Miss Trotter, who had artistic proclivities, sketches him as he appears in the print.

It will be observed that his dress is very similar to O'Hampsay's.

Referring to the clothing of the harpers at Belfast, Bunting says : "They were in general clad in a comfortable homely manner, in drab-coloured or grey cloth of coarse manufacture."

A few of them made an attempt at splendour, by wearing silver buttons on their coats. Arthur O'Neill, who claimed descent from the illustrious family of that name, had his initials surmounted by the device of Ulster (a right hand) engraved on silver buttons the size of half a crown. It is recorded that the beautiful harp in the library of Trinity College, Dublin, was played by O'Neill through the streets of Limerick in 1760.

This is the oldest known harp and is popularly known as " King Brian Borou's," but Dr. Petrie puts its origin not earlier than the fourteenth or fifteenth century and, therefore, it could not have been Brian Borou's, who was killed at the battle of Clontarf in 1014. It is probably one of the small harps used by the Irish monks in their religious worship. The initials " I.H.S." are carved on it, which strengthens the idea of its being used in the worship of the church.

There is a small silver shield attached to the forearm with the arms of O'Neill engraved on it, i.e., a right hand with two quaint dogs as supporters, from which Dr. Petrie thinks it most probably belonged to one of two O'Neills who flourished in the fourteenth century, one as Bishop of Clogher and the other as Bishop of Derry.

It is from this harp that we derive the now universally accepted typical shape, which, for art purposes, has quite displaced the old angelic form.

PATRICK QUINN
1745-1812

Whatever may have been the costume of the bards of old, it is improbable that it was a "uniform" in the sense we understand that term; the essential distinguishing feature would be the harp itself.

The Irish MSS. however, are not yet exhausted, and further research may reveal additional details as to the costume of the Irish Harpers.

THE "TRINITY COLLEGE" HARP

COSTUME OF THE IRISH PIPER

By Samuel Leighton

With illustrations by the Author

" The bagpipe was known in Ireland from very early times; the form used was that commonly known as the Highland pipes—slung from the shoulder, the bag inflated from the mouth.

The other form—resting on the lap, the bag inflated by a bellows—is much the finer instrument, but of modern invention."

P. W. Joyce, M.R.I.A.

The bagpipe is a very old, primitive instrument. In its earliest form, it consisted of a windbag in which two tubes were inserted, one to blow through with the mouth in order to fill the bag with wind, and the other was pierced with a few holes, forming what we know as a chanter, upon which simple melodies could be played.

It appears to have been in use both in the East and the West. In England it was used by the shepherds as a pastoral pipe and has always been a favourite amongst the Irish and Scotch Celts from very remote times.

A very quaint illustration showing associa- tion between a pig and the bagpipe appears in an ancient Irish MS. (Dinnseanchus) of A.D. 544, in the British Museum. It forms part of an initial letter at the com- mencement of one of the chapters. The interweaving of fanciful forms of animals and birds is customary in Irish illumina- tions, but the introduction of the pig is very unusual. It is, however, evidence of the antiquity of the bagpipe with two drones. The pig presses the bag against his belly with his foreleg.

"THE PIG AND PIPES"
Copied from Bunting's
"Ancient Music of Ireland"

" And from his lungs into the bag is blown
Supply of needful air to feed the growling drone."

E. Bunting.

At the Welsh Eisteddfod at Caerwys in 1100, King Griffith, in order to in- troduce the Irish bagpipes, gave particular prominence to pipe performances, and we read in the Welsh annals that "the prize was carried off by an Irish- man, who received from the Monarch a silver pipe as a reward for his skill."

The pipes were common to the Scotch and Irish, and during the early warlike times, always accompanied the military expeditions. The Irish war pipe (Piob Mor) was very similar to the Highland pipe with which we are familiar to this day.

J. Derricke, in his " Image of Ireland " (1581), supplies us with an illus- tration of a war party of Kernes headed by a piper playing a very large set of pipes. The drawing is very coarse, but it serves to show the style, not only of the pipes, but also of the dress of the period.

This is a very fierce barbaric group on the war path, with the piper at their head. He is shown with the long hanging sleeves, falling lower than the knees, he carried a sword and wears armlets. The hair is worn long, as was customary, and all are bareheaded. The Kernes, or peasants, cherished a bitter animosity towards the Anglo-Norman invaders, and deliberately refused to adopt their fashion in clothes. In fighting, they went almost naked, a habit which lost them many a battle, as it placed them at a disadvantage to their mail-clad foes. A man with a hat was looked upon with contempt, as a "Saxon beau." The English adopted the conquerors' style of dress, but for centuries, the Irish maintained their national costume.

"IRISH KERNES AND PIPER"
From J. Derricke's "Image of Ireland" (1581)

The Kernes in the illustration wear a short kilt-like coat, slashed at the shoulders, with a waist band pleated, in folds.

> " Their skirtes be very strange,
> Not reaching past the thigh,
> With pleates on pleates they pleated are
> As thick as pleates they lie :
> Whose slieves hang trailing downe
> Almost under the shoe,
> And with a mantle commonlie
> The Irish Kerne doeth goe."   J. DERRICKE.

The piper wore a similar dress, but it is largely hidden by the bag of the pipes. This instrument is admitted to have been the proper military music of the Irish, shortly before the treaty of Limerick (1691).

The music of the Kerne in the reign of Edward III was the bagpipes. I cannot find any evidence of the bagpiper having any distinctive costume as such, at this period, and it seems most likely that he was dressed as the others—plus the pipes, which gave him sufficient distinction amongst his fellows.

" The bagpipe is not mentioned in connexion with the kings or nobles, and must have been entirely confined to the peasants, even long after the Anglo-Norman invasion. It appears to have begun to be used in war in the fourteenth century, but there is no evidence that it was ever so used by the Irish, even before the advent of the Normans."

" An old Irish MS., thus refers to the costume of the pipers : ' I saw there,' said Ingcel, 'a couch and nine persons upon it; they had fair yellow hair, and were like in beauty; they wore speckled, glossy cloaks, and had nine ornamental quadrangular caps (*tennes*) over them. The emblazonment which is upon these quadrangular caps, would be suffic-ient light for the royal house. These are the nine pipe-players who came from the fairy hills of Bregia to Conaire to do him honour. They are the best pipe-players in the whole world.' "

O'CURRY, (Vol, III, p. 139).

The long cloak was common to all grades of society, varying chiefly in the value of the material and decoration. Giraldus Cambrensis tells us that " The Irish wear their woollen clothes mostly black, because the sheep of Ireland are in general of that colour. The dress itself is of a barbarous fashion. They wear moderate close-cowled or hooded mantles (*caputiis*), which spread over their shoulders and reach down to the elbow, composed of small pieces of cloths of different kinds and colours, for the most part sewed together, beneath which woollen fallins (*phalinges*) instead of a cloak, or breeches and stockings in one piece, and these generally dyed of some colour." This description has reference to the twelfth century.

" In 1562 Shane O'Neill, Prince of Ulster, appeared at the court of Eliza-beth with his guards of Galloglachs, bareheaded, barelegged, and armed with hatchets, their hair flowing in locks on their shoulders, attired in shirts dyed with saffron, their sleeves large, their tunics short, and their cloaks shagged." (CAMDEN—Hist. Elizabeth.)

As a picture of an Ulsterman of the invincible type, this is interesting, both for costume and personality.

We have here an illustration said to be " Drawn after the Quicke " (from life) in which we find the full plaited skirts with long trailing sleeves hanging down, as described by Derricke, the short coat and jacket with half sleeves, very short waisted, embroidered, and legs bare. The skene (short sword) in his hand suggests a warrior, of a higher grade then the Kerne, whose clothes are of a simpler character, frequently nothing but a simple garment in the form of a capacious cloak, which covers his nakedness by day, and in which he sleeps on the ground by night. In this illustration, if we substitute a set of pipes for the formidable short sword, we may easily recognise in it a true variant

"EARLY IRISH COSTUME"
Copied from a very rare engraving of
Irish Costume in the Bodleian Library,
Oxford (Douse Collection)

of the ancient picturesque costume of the Irish piper of a better class than the Kerne.

The Scottish Highlanders are famous both in peace and in war for their use of pipes, and this has had a considerable influence on the costume of the piper. No Highland honours as such are considered complete without the pipes, not even the bringing in of the haggis at a Burns's dinner. In 1746 a piper named James Reid was executed at York as a rebel, it was advanced in his favour that he did not carry a sword, but the court held " That a Highland regiment never marched without a piper, and therefore his bagpipe in the eyes of the law was an instrument of war."

The Highland kilt was not adopted by the Scotch till about the eighteenth century. The earliest portrait of a Highland chief in which the kilt is represented, was painted in 1746 and is in possession of the family of Glengarry of Inveree. It is the portrait of Alexander MacDonnell and his henchman; the latter alone wears the kilt, which was at that time a sign of servitude.

The following gives us an insight into the use of the bagpipes and their popularity with the people.

A traveller had taken refuge from the rain in the shelter of a humble cottage, the home of an old couple near Killarney; on being asked how she intended to support her family, the old mother said : " Some of them will go out to service, one or two will help me on the land, and as for Donough, my eldest boy, who was blinded by the small-pox, we have got a man to teach him the bagpipes, there is no fear, with the help of God, he will get an honest livelihood and live comfortably; at any rate, it will be better than being a sorry tradesman."

When Donough is ready for the road, his costume will not trouble his mother very much.

The modern Irish pipe is a very different instrument from the war pipe. A small bellows under the arm has been substituted for the mouth, the drones have had keys added so that a chord can be sounded at will, in addition to the music of the chanter. A soft effect also is produced by dropping the end of the chanter upon a band of leather tied round the leg above the knee. This is the present form of the Irish pipes called " Uillean," the old one being the war pipe or Piob Mor.

PLATE XXXV

CHARLES RICKETTS, A.R.A.
For W. B. Yeats' " King's Threshold."
Abbey Theatre, Dublin.

PLATE XXXVI

CHARLES RICKETTS, A.R.A.
For W. B. Yeats' " King's Threshold."
Abbey Theatre, Dublin.

PLATE XXXVII

NORAH McGUINNESS
" Deirdre."
For W. B. Yeats' " Deirdre."
Abbey Theatre, Dublin

PLATE XXXVIII

NORAH McGUINNESS
" Fergus."
For W. B. Yeats' " Deirdre."
Abbey Theatre, Dublin.

PLATE XXXIX

NORAH McGUINNESS
"Nessa."
For W. B. Yeats' "Deirdre."
Abbey Theatre, Dublin.

PLATE XXXIX

NORAH McGUINNESS
" Naise."
For W. B. Yeats' " Deirdre."
Abbey Theatre, Dublin.

PLATE XL.

NORAH McGUINNESS
"Musician."
For W. B. Yeats' "Deirdre,"
Abbey Theatre, Dublin.

PLATE XL

NORAH McGUINNESS
" Musician."
For W. B. Yeats' " Deirdre."
Abbey Theatre, Dublin.

PLATE XLI

LAURENCE BRADSHAW
" Banshee."
For W. B. Yeats' " Hawk's Well."

PLATE XLII

R. BOYD MORRISON
" Chief Irish Harper."
For Gerald Macnamara's " Thompson in Tír-na-n'-Óg."
Ulster Players, Belfast.

PLATE XLIII

R. BOYD MORRISON

"Grania"

For Gerald Macnamara's "Thompson in Tír-na-n-Óg"

Ulster Players, Belfast.

PLATE XLIII

R. BOYD MORRISON
" Grania."
For Gerald Macnamara's " Thompson in Tír-na-n'-Óg."
Ulster Players, Belfast.

"GRANIA"

COSTUME DESIGN

"THOMPSON IN TIR-NA-N'OG"
GERALD MACNAMARA
ULSTER PLAYERS.
BELFAST.

Boyd Morrison
1925-26-27

PLATE XLIV

R. BOYD MORRISON
" Harper."
For Gerald Macnamara's " Thompson in Tír-na-n'-Óg."
Ulster Players, Belfast.

1867 HARPER

R. Boyd Morrison
1976

PLATE XLV

R. BOYD MORRISON
" Cuchulain."
For Gerald Macnamara's " Thompson in Tír-na-n'-Óg."
Ulster Players, Belfast.

Cuchulain of the Ford

R. Boyd Morrin
1874

PLATE XLVI

WILLIAM CONOR
For Gerald Macnamara's " Thompson in Tír-na-n'-Óg."
Ulster Players, Belfast.

PLATE XLVII

WILLIAM CONOR
" Nance."
For Richard Rowley's " The Last Coyne of Killehalla."
Northern Drama League, Belfast.

PLATE XLVIII

WILLIAM CONOR
For Peter Maginnes' " The Old Women."

PLATE XLIX

WILLIAM CONOR
For Richard Rowley's " The Last Coyne of Killehalla."
Northern Drama League, Belfast

PLATE L

WILLIAM CONOR
For Rutherford Mayne's " The Drone."

IV
COSTUME

COSTUME

By Sir Barry V. Jackson, M.A.

FOUNDER AND DIRECTOR OF THE BIRMINGHAM REPERTORY THEATRE

I cannot help feeling that the editors of this handsome and welcome volume have been actuated by a slight touch of malice in asking me to contribute to their pages an appreciation of the value of costume on the stage.

A short time ago I was responsible for presenting to a horrified world a production of Shakespeare's " Hamlet " in which all the traditional costume and setting was swept away and the characters of the great tragedy, clad in the garments of to-day, moved and spoke as our contemporaries might in such conditions. I must refer to this because it was at once assumed that I was not a believer in the accurate and beautiful costuming of imaginative plays and wished to dispense in every case with these important adjuncts to the drama. The production was criticised not only in this country by those who saw it, but also thousands of miles away by those who had not seen and, therefore, disbelieved—their judgment presumably being all the more unbiassed because they had no facts to embarrass their speculations. I think I may say that the majority of those who saw the modern version, though they might disapprove of details, enjoyed it as a whole, and it was at once assumed that in future all productions of Shakespeare and other classical works would be given in this less decorative style. Incidentally, it was also assumed that a production of this kind was necessarily cheaper to stage; this turned out to be an illusion, which indeed we had never fostered ourselves.

Our friends the public and the press were more carried away by the success in practice of the new method—or rather revival of an old method familiar to our stage until the nineteenth century renaissance of archæological interest—than we were ourselves, and while we hope to repeat the experiment as successfully with other Shakespeare plays, it by no means follows that we should wish to do it as a rule. During the fourteen years of the Birmingham Repertory Theatre's existence, we have experimented in every possible way with the production of plays by Shakespeare and what may be generally termed " costume plays " of every kind. So far, we have only applied the modern method to three out of several score, namely " Cymbeline" "Hamlet," and "All's Well That Ends Well," which seemed to us to lend themselves particularly well to such treatment. We have also produced Shakespeare in frankly fantastic form, again with plain historical accuracy, again with some attempt at rough symbolism.

While I am convinced that the essentials of drama are simple and universal—that is what we set out to prove by the " modern clothes Hamlet " —and sometimes remember with longing the famous French epigram which declares that all that is necessary to a great play is " four boards and a great passion "—which may be true either of a very primitive world or of a very perfect one—there can be no doubt that of the manifold arts which unite to form the compound art of the stage, the designing of appropriate and beautiful costume is one of the most attractive both to the artist concerned and to the spectator.

The incidents of the plot and its further implications of moral teaching, of satire, or of romance, the beauty or wit of the language, the living plastic pictures that the actors form upon the stage, the communal emotion of the spectators, these are and must always be the important things of the drama; they *are* the drama. There is no need to insist on presenting these essentials stripped of all the added beauties which the artist can confer upon them when means are adequate. But we must remember the essential. Often little bands of amateur players come to me and say, " We should like to act such and such a play, but how can we afford the costumes and scenery needed? " The only answer to this is that they are not *needed*, greatly though they may be desired. If a play is worth acting, one can dispense with the ornaments of production; if it is not, no amount of beautiful dresses and scenes, admirable in themselves, can make of it a work of art.

It may seem strange that in a book devoted to the praise of the designer, I should emphasise so strongly that his art is an adjunct to, and not an essential of the stage. It is precisely because I hold the art of stage-design in such high esteem that I wish to make very clear what the position of the designer in the theatre should be. The fatal tendency, fatal alike to the play and to the designs, is to exaggerate the importance of dress and scene. The play can become overloaded with a cargo of fripperies and the artist will have failed in the chief duty of every artist—to work towards perfection within the due limits which that art entails upon him. It is a platitude to point out that the sculptor who tries to copy the realistic detail of painted portraiture, or the dainty charm of an ivory miniature, the architect in stone who apes the fretted elaboration of carven wood, the artist in any medium who, while extracting every ounce of which his medium is capable, does not realise the bounds of his art, and work the better for their discipline, is not a true artist at all. The proof lies in the great artists of the past who have felt and benefited by such control. If this is true of the major arts, how much more of the applied arts, whose very name signifies their ancillary character? The sculptor who is called in to carve a frieze in relief upon a great building is proud to subordinate his part of the work to the general line and character of the whole, and feels success only in proportion as he does so. Similarly the stage-designer must feel that he is but one of many working to a common end, and be proud of striking one note in a concord rather than of executing a brilliant individual flourish which may jar with the remainder.

The artists whose work is represented in this book will in all probability smile with a mixture of pity and impatience because they themselves, fully realising the truth and importance of these strictures, have never transgressed them. I am addressing rather those to whom this book, with its garnered experience of designers and producers, will be of supreme value, the countless young artists who are looking towards the stage as an outlet for expression. One sees their work in exhibitions, it is submitted daily to producers. In a very large proportion of their work, it is clear that they have not felt the necessity for discipline and subordination. In many cases, this is due to inability to get that practical experience, in a theatre, or on one of the more elaborate amateur productions, which is so necessary to develop their art along these lines. The opportunities unfortunately are much fewer than the applicants. They can, however, when visiting theatres, observe very closely the way in which the problems of scene, costume and lighting have been handled, detect mistakes of over-emphasis, and endeavour to feel the play as one texture of woven strands, not as an excuse for " working-in " the designer's independent ideas.

It is, of course, the producer's business to preserve harmony between the various parts of the spectacle to be given, and though the artist, just like the actor, may sometimes feel that jealousy, shortsightedness or pure ignorance have led to the alteration or abolition of some part of his work, he is probably wrong. The producer knows best nine times out of ten; he has the talent and the training to take a more general view than either artist or actor. Moreover, he will often suggest new ideas to the artist, just as something in the designs may alter for the better his own conception. The two will work together hand in hand and ensure that fitness which is the aim of both.

Another thing that both should work together to ensure is economy. In theatrical production, though it is hard to believe it when managers boast in the Press of the sums expended on a given spectacle, there is no virtue in extravagance. Wherever an effect can be gained as well by a less as by a greater expenditure, it should be so gained, and the costume designer, often a sinner in this respect, should use a reasonable amount of ingenuity in getting his effects with the least waste. Theatrical expenses to-day are very high, and not the least of them is the one that concerns us here, the high cost of materials and labour needed for costume. Now it is as important for the costume artist as for everyone connected with the management of the theatre at this moment to remove the danger which besets the theatre, and renders it an easy prey to the proportionally much cheaper entertainment of the cinematograph. The heavy expenses the theatre has to face, in London at any rate, make it essential to charge prices far in advance of the cinemas; it is therefore less popular, and the taking of risks much less possible. Productions which do not succeed from the outset are in almost every case doomed to failure, and the unlucky manager may be driven from business into bankruptcy, all the more readily if he has had to incur heavy initial expenses on the production which even with good receipts many weeks would be needed to wipe off. If economy is an important virtue in the professional theatres of a big city, it is the hinge of success in the performances of amateur bodies who have no great financial backing, play for a few nights only to limited audiences, and have to make both ends meet or vanish out of existence. And it is to these amateur bodies that we must now in great part look for the life-blood of the theatre, the sense of adventure which will make discoveries. Every pound off their bills frees them for more and better work.

It does not follow that the results of practising economy will be at all inferior to those where the designer and maker of the costumes are given "carte blanche." Greater simplicity of design more often leads to beauty than the reverse, and a knowledge and use of simpler materials discovers effects which may even surpass those gained by more expensive ones. Indeed in stage conditions, the latter are often noticed to fail of their effect, while the cheaper, rightly used, appear much richer. It is not, as some designers think, always necessary to get real silks and brocades at an incredible price per yard. Just as the life of a king can be represented on the stage in three hours, his robes can often be represented by three shillings. It is all part of the illusion which is the theatre.

I have put these things first—discipline and economy—because, as I have said, they are the two things in which the designer may most often be found to fail. There is little need to say more of them. When found in close conjunction with these two virtues, the requirements of his craft are those of any other graphic art : a sense of line as embodied particularly in a feeling for drapery and pattern; a sense of colour made more practical by a knowledge of the effects of stage lights upon it and more significant by a feeling for the emotional and the symbolic values of colour; invention and originality; and to balance them, a knowledge of and understanding of the past, useful in every art as a source of fresh inspiration, and as a check to extravagances, and necessary to this art in particular where an accurate representation both of archæological detail and of the general spirit of a bygone age are so frequently demanded.

One point should be emphasised. This book deals with the art of the designer of costumes and there is room for hundreds of others devoted to this side of the designer's art alone. It should not be forgotten, however, that the man who designs the costumes should also design the scenic background against which they are to be shown, otherwise discrepancies of colour, form, and feeling, are sure to arise. The costumes and the scenery should be treated as one whole, and though it is convenient to treat of them separately, since there is so much to be said about both, it is necessary to remember their intimate relation. The producer, the designer, will have in their minds certain groupings and pictures which will occur at striking moments of the play, and which can only be realised if the same artist has directed the whole. It may interest the reader if we turn from these general considerations to some particular productions which we have done at the Birmingham Repertory Theatre. It is with Shakespeare particularly that most costume designers get their chance, and as I mentioned above we have experimented with the costuming of Shakespeare productions along several different lines. In "The Tempest," for instance, we adopted a rough symbolism of colour, the island and its inhabitants, Prospero, Caliban and Miranda were painted and dressed in varying tones of blue which distinguished them from the intruding members of the Ship's company who were clad in reds and browns.

In "Much Ado about Nothing" which was produced for us very cleverly by Mr. Conal O'Riordan we used an almost entirely white architectural background; the characters were dressed from designs by Guy Kortright in black, red and yellow. The contrast gave an effect of hard brilliancy which seemed to reproduce entirely the atmosphere of the play with its keen dazzling wit, and the sharp distinction between the good and evil characters, which was further emphasised by the colouring of the costumes; this was not of course carried to too great an extreme. The same plan was used to a certain extent by Mr. Paul Shelving in his designs for "The Immortal Hour" where the two spiritual planes of the play were clearly marked, the immortal characters being dressed in a shimmering green and silver in contrast with the earthly scarlet, gold and yellow of the mortals. Naturally, this method must be used with tact or it might become ridiculous and imperil the message of the play by too obvious differentiation between the various characters. We have also produced others of Shakespeare plays, notably the chronicle plays with as close an attention to historical accuracy as was possible, using a very simple and rapidly changed background and concentrating for colour on the costumes themselves.

I cannot speak warmly enough of the work of Mr. Paul Shelving who has designed practically all our scenes and costumes for the last six years; an indefatigable worker and eager student, an artist with a fine sense of colour and, as is nowhere more apparent than in black and white photographs of his work, a master of effective line. He has had to face problems of every kind with very little relaxation, since we produce a new play every fortnight; whether it be a rural comedy, a fantastic setting for a play by Molière, a reproduction of a mediæval stage for a mystery play, he is almost invariably successful. Perhaps one of the high-water marks of his achievement was the setting and costumes for the first part of Bernard Shaw's " Back to Methusalah" which has rarely been rivalled in modern times.

It is certainly one of the few things on which the stage of to-day may congratulate itself that, more and more it is seeking the assistance of the real artist in the theatre. At one time the preparations for the scenery and costumes were left partly to chance and partly to people without the necessary talent to make the best of their opportunities. This infiltration of the artist into the theatre should be continued with might and main. It might seem that at the moment, mainly through economic reasons, the theatre is not so popular a form of entertainment as it was thirty years ago, but there are many signs that the period of depression is passing. It is already very obvious in the provinces, where people who cannot get what they want out of the professional theatres are doing things for themselves, and achieving admirable results. The weight of their influence will make itself felt on the professional theatre, and there will be more and more opportunities for the real artist of every kind. This book no doubt will be eagerly studied by many young people who will, in ten or twenty years time, give us something remarkable, and should be very grateful to the pioneer work of the artists whose designs are reproduced here which, beautiful in themselves, are perhaps even more valuable as an inspiration to the future.

PAUL SHELVING

PLATE LI

PAUL SHELVING
For Lord Dunsany's " The Queen's Enemies."
Birmingham Repertory Theatre.

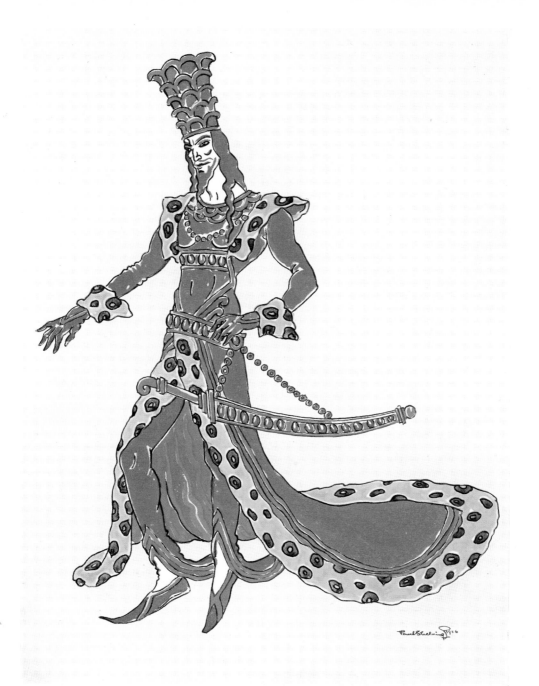

PLATE LII

PAUL SHELVING
Costume and Mask for Magician, " Coq d'Or."
Birmingham Repertory Theatre

Paul Scheurich 1926.

PLATE LIII

PAUL SHELVING
Mask and Costume for a Turk (Masquerade).
Molière's " Le Bourgeois Gentilhomme."
Birmingham Repertory Theatre.

PLATE **LIV**

PAUL SHELVING
A Masker.
For Reginald Somerville's " David Garrick.'
Birmingham Repertory Theatre.

V
COSTUME AT THE LYRIC THEATRE HAMMERSMITH

COSTUME AT THE LYRIC THEATRE HAMMERSMITH—I

By Nigel Playfair

It is impossible, or at least inadvisable, to give an account of the costumes made use of in the various productions of this Theatre without first outlining very briefly the general principles which have up to now governed its policy. From the first moment of its control by myself and my fellow-directors, to quote one of them, Mr. Arnold Bennett, " No piece has been given which we did not unanimously believe to have considerable artistic merit." And from the first play to the present, no costume has been seen upon the stage which has not been either designed and specially made, or passed for approval—if by chance it has been bought ready-made or hired —by an artist whom we believed to have the right expert knowledge as to its suitability in relation to the production as a whole.

Moreover, after the first production we have learnt the lesson and profited by it—that all costumes for a play must be under the control of the same artist who has designed the scenery and supervised the lighting arrangements.

It is necessary to add that from the beginning the most rigid economy has been necessary and this has entailed a very careful study of the economy of means in creating an effect—an economy not only in the actual materials used, but in the elimination of trimmings, and the substitution of suggestion for realism. Some such sort of economy has, with few exceptions, been found necessary in all the theatres of Europe, since the general exchequer found itself everywhere in strained circumstances after the war. But, perhaps, this particular theatre furnishes a very favourable and concrete example. I think it will be granted that the various experiments made have

M

proved that the necessity is not without its compensating advantages, if only because it has confirmed the fact, that the general standard of good taste can only be kept up where the presence of the creative artist can make itself felt—that the gorgeousness and richness which were the key-note of theatrical production in mid-Victorian times are really a very poor substitute for ingenuity and inspiration.

It will be seen by a glance at the list of plays which have been given at this theatre during the present regime that there has existed every opportunity for such ingenuity, and for every variety of taste and method :—

" Make Believe."
*" The Younger Generation." ⎱
" La Serva Padrona." ⎰ Double Bill.
" Abraham Lincoln."
*" John Ferguson."
" As You Like it."
" The Beggar's Opera."
" Merry Wives of Windsor."
" The Way of the World."
" Midsummer Madness."
" The Duenna."
" The Rivals."
*" The Cherry Orchard."
*" And That's the Truth (If you think it is)."
" Lionel and Clarissa."
" Riverside Nights."

I purposely do not say much, if anything, about the costumes used in the plays marked in this list with an asterisk, because they are modern plays, calling for no special notes of interest upon the costume. I deal almost entirely with the plays belonging to a period before our own—with what may be roughly called " historical costume."

There are three ways of setting about the creation of such historical dresses. One may start in a strictly archæological mood, determining that the dresses shall be an absolute replica of what was worn in the period dealt with—the same in design, the same in colour, the same in cut, and the same in material. This was the ideal of the school of producers founded in England, at any rate, by Charles Kean, and continued throughout the Irving and Tree epochs.

There is a second method, by which strict accuracy may be disregarded, and the decorative aspect only insisted upon.

And thirdly, we may combine the two, and while admitting nothing in the way of shape or cut which is not strictly accurate, still allow ourselves a certain latitude in colour, decoration and general detail. This has been the principle mostly adopted at the Lyric Theatre, Hammersmith, and is, I think, the method most suitable to the theatre generally; for in the theatre the main object is to create a momentary illusion. The picture or the pageant does not remain so long before the eyes that people have the leisure or inclination to question the accuracy of the details; and, of course, even if they had, only a very limited number of them have either the knowledge or the desire to do so.

Moreover, it is not true that such a method allows the shirking of responsibility, or makes the task of the designer or supervisor any more easy; on the contrary, really it adds to his difficulties, for a photographically accurate reproduction of a dress, provided authorities are available—as they usually are—is obviously less difficult than the creation of a general illusion. To take liberties with costumes, to be picturesquely inaccurate, in fact, means that one must be steeped in the feeling and spirit of an age which is not one's own. Any designer who works, and works successfully, in this method, must really, as it were, acquire the feeling and spirit possessed by the designers of that particular period.

I think it can be broadly laid down as a general principle that the first, or archæological, method seldom or never has a lasting effect from a stage point of view, and that simply because of its stark reality, and for this very simple reason—that real dresses were designed for real people, engaged in doing the real things of life, and not for being exhibited in the artificial light of a stage and surrounded with a painted idealisation.

You must remember always that costumes for the stage are designed not only to be seen in a certain light, but at a certain distance—that too much detail is apt to blur their colour and to dull their edges. It is the shape of a dress, its line and its cut, that are of paramount importance in creating the necessary illusion; ornament and detail need to be most sparingly used.

The second method which I spoke of—the method which takes no account of accuracy, but simply improvises variations on the fashions of a particular period, has not been made very much use of at the Lyric Theatre, for the simple reason that it is merely suitable to plays of pure fantasy, and not many of these have been given at this theatre. There have been, however, two exceptions. One of these was the children's play, called " Make Believe," and the other was the little light opera called " Midsummer Madness."

The first of these had for its characters children, fairytale folk, and pirates. Obviously the more fantastically they were dressed, the better the result established. It is true enough that in real life no fifteenth century woodcutter would ever have met a princess dressed as our princess was in the first act; she belonged to no period at all, but was simply a fairytale princess created from a child's imagination—a child who might have seen a dozen pictures of princesses belonging to all centuries, from the early Greek to our own and had, as it were, combined all the information he or she had acquired from them in a fantastic and composite costume. The woodcutter who fell in love with her happened to wear a fifteenth-century tunic and hood simply because in this case the child would think at once of a particular picture, of a particular wood-cutter that he had seen in some old book; and because the dress was simple, he would remember it whole and complete. In the same way, the little servants and pages had their dresses designed to follow the characters in a pack of cards; for no child who has handled cards is ever likely to think that courtiers can be very suitably dressed otherwise.

The same principles applied to Mr. George Sheringham's designs for " Midsummer Madness." They were purely whimsical in their conception, though obviously they descended from the conventionalised masques of the Italian Commedia dell' Arte; and because the play was intended to take place roughly in our own times, though in our own times fantasticated and made definitely picturesque, Mr. Sheringham very cleverly combined with them a very attractive mixture of pseudo-Victorian fashions which fitted admirably the airy texture of the whole comedy.

The method that I have advocated as being the best in dealing with period costumes was the one almost invariably followed by the late Claude Lovat Fraser. He had, as a matter of fact, an almost unrivalled knowledge of the details of costume of every period. Before setting to work on any particular play he would steep himself in the atmosphere of the period to be represented, reading every book he could lay his hands upon on that period, looking at every picture or illustration from that period, studying contemporary portraits—and to such an extent that, before he began his actual work, he would really feel himself to be living in the particular century that was being dealt with. But when he had done all this work, he would never, in making his designs, copy any particular picture or pay strict attention to any particular description of a dress. What he tried to do, and what he succeeded in doing, was to think, himself, in terms of the chosen period, to design his dresses as if he were indeed himself a contemporary of the people in the play to be decorated, and not as if he were a modern painter reconstructing a bygone era. He held that only thus could a living and truly dramatic thing be created out of the past, and he wished his work to be as distinct as possible from a mere piece of museum reconstruction, which he always thought utterly unsuitable to the needs of a theatre, and especially of a theatre in which space is as restricted as that of the stage of the Lyric Theatre, Hammersmith.

I don't mean by this that he was indifferent to accuracy; but he contended —and I think rightly contended—that true accuracy must proceed from the inner consciousness of the artist. So successful was his method that once he set to work it was impossible for him to introduce into any of his designs anything that was really inaccurate or anachronistic. He would at once feel instinctively if a mistake were made that a jarring note had been struck in his entire design. It was from him, indeed, that I learnt so much of that elimination of unnecessary detail of which I have already spoken. It was only in his later productions that he carried out his theories in this direction to the full, and particularly in regard to his most famous and most successful designs which were made for " The Beggar's Opera." I think it is true that he would begin his work with a very carefully thought-out colour-scheme for the play as a whole; and it was a favourite theory of his that every period of dress had in it a kind of architecture which gave it its entire character and flavour.

By this he meant that the shapes of the sleeves, the size of the head-dresses, were the logical and inevitable outcome of the shape of a dress as a whole; and that once the shape had been settled, very drastic simplification might be indulged in without losing the real vital essence of the period. For instance, the ladies of the town in " The Beggar's Opera " all wore their hair dressed exactly alike, all their foreheads were completely bared, and the shape of their hair-dressing presented a picture of the small, sleek head with its formal side-puffs which not only is characteristic of the early eighteenth-century, but is the inevitable head-dressing to match the wide panniers with flat backs and fronts, which are in direct contrast to the round bell-hoops and towering head-dresses of the later half of the century.

And why, you might very well ask, did these ladies all wear their hair exactly alike, when in reality a set of women of the sort, collected together in a real tavern at this period, would probably have shown very considerable variations? The answer is, of course, that by using the same shape in masses you insist on and underline the general characteristic of the period; the eye, in fact, is purposely centred on a particular effect.

The same rule applies to the dresses, in which everything in the way of flowered and figured materials was avoided, simply because the designer wished to create a very clean, hard and unsentimental colour-scheme in keeping with the general character of the play. The broad main lines of the designs—the hoops, wigs, hats, shoes, and the very wide-cuffed sleeves, were absolutely correct by historical examples; but once he had established the accurate effect, the designer very allowably gave his fancy full play.

It is curious but true that in a previous play which Lovat Fraser designed and in which he kept with far more meticulous fidelity to his period, altering and simplifying very little, he found his efforts in this direction met with a very curious reward. This play was " As You Like It," the designs for which Lovat Fraser chose to take from the early fifteenth century as a suitable setting. He chose it because its very elaboration, its fantastic head-dresses, and its clean, jewel-like colours seemed to him to express the spirit of the play very perfectly. In the designs which he made, he differentiated very carefully between the elaboration of the Court and the weather-worn linens of the country folk; in fact, he put the exiled Duke and his followers into what he called " the Norfolk jacket and grey flannel trousers of the period." But the usurping Duke's Court wore clothes heavily patterned with gold and vermilion, robes elaborately cut and slashed, great fantastic head-dresses, heelless shoes with long soft points, and tight silken hose. The ladies of the Court showed not a vestige of hair, and Fraser even insisted on their painting out their eyebrows to simulate the fashion of plucking them out which was then in vogue. The exiled Court and the peasants, on the other hand, were dressed in linens of soft vegetable colours (a great many of the materials used were actually dyed with saffron), and, instead of the tight Court hose, wore the much looser cloth coverings bound round with coloured thongs, which were, of course, a survival of a much earlier period.

In this he made use of another piece of knowledge, which is that no period is quite definitely clean-cut and separated from the rest, but that unfashionable or unfortunate folk carry over to a certain extent the clothes of their earlier years into later life; so that the fashions in the mass of the people merge imperceptibly into one another, and really only a comparatively small and wealthy minority are always up-to-date and the last word of the mode, so to speak. It is interesting to note how far this is true in different periods —how far more quickly, for instance, fashions change in periods of prosperity than in periods of stress and excitement.

The effect, however, on the public mind of this very faithful reproduction of a period very little made use of by modern archæologically minded painters and designers was unexpected. Instead of Fraser being congratulated on his accurate reproduction, he was thought to have quite illegitimately invented a fantastic scheme; and there was hardly a critic who did not put down the whole production as a bad example of the strained and futurist tendencies of twentieth-century artists !

Besides " As You Like It " and " The Beggar's Opera," Fraser also designed the dresses for the eighteenth-century Pergolesi's " La Serva Padrona "; and here his dresses were the eighteenth century quite frankly fantasticated and even caricatured, but caricatured not as a modern painter would caricature the eighteenth century, but from the point of view of a contemporary caricaturist. Moreover, in their bright colours they suggested, and rightly, Italy and not England.

The other principal designers who have worked for this theatre have been Miss Doris Zinkeisen, Mr. George Sheringham and Mr. Norman Wilkinson. I don't think that any of these three differ very much in their general outlook from Mr. Lovat Fraser; but they differ very much indeed in their actual designs, for they are all three individual artists with a personality of their own. And, of course, it is part of the delight of a theatre to recognise the personality of the artist in the costumes and scenery which he provides.

I think Miss Zinkeisen was a particularly happy choice to illustrate the sparkle and wit of Congreve's dialogue. Certainly in the very beautiful dress of Millamant you will see a certain youthfulness and spontaneity; but all the same she has preserved the general lines of her period with perfect accuracy; and it cannot be too much insisted upon that besides giving a reproduction of the dresses of a period, it is a designer's duty to help to emphasise the particular character which an actor or actress has to portray. How much this was realised by the designers of one of the best periods of the English theatre, you can see by a study of the pictures of such a great artist as Zoffany. It was the foolish practice of the minor critics of a few years back to sneer at that period—to imagine that because Garrick, for example, acted Hamlet in a wig and an eighteenth-century Court suit, the whole art of stage designing was in an elementary and inefficient condition. If anybody thinks this to be a real truth, let him look one after another at two pictures—Zoffany's, of a scene in " Venice Preserved," now in the possession of the Garrick Club, and a picture by John Collier painted in the early part of this century from " The Merry Wives of Windsor "— also to be seen in the same place. I am not saying for a moment that Collier's is a bad picture; on the contrary, it is one of the very best examples of that artist's work. It presents a scene upon which the memory of anyone who witnessed it dwells with delight; the dresses are accurate, and in their way quite good. In Zoffany's picture the anachronism in the costumes is obvious; but on the other hand, no unprejudiced observer who is fond of the theatre could doubt for one moment which scene is pictorially the more effective, and no more striking example of the superiority of imagination in design over the methods of realism could possibly be quoted.

This is not to say, of course, that richness of material is in itself a disadvantage. That would obviously be merely another case of calling " sour grapes." For hot-house grapes, for most of the unfortunate rent-ridden managements, rich materials have become. They present a danger only when their richness tempts the designers to depend upon that quality rather than their own imagination. Otherwise the opportunity for using them may often give rise to a very legitimate envy on the part of those who are denied their use.

And there are certain costume designers who superimpose upon their own inspiration richness of material with dazzling and beautiful effect. I am particularly thinking as I write of one of our greatest designers, Mr. Ricketts. He is able to work in simple material with great success—his costumes for " Judith " at the Kingsway may be remembered in this connection; but when he can really command silks and velvets he is at his very perfect best.

I have spoken a little of Mr. Sheringham's designs for " Midsummer Madness." In " The Duenna " he gave another example of the successful treatment of a fantastic eighteenth-century play—a play, of course, belonging to a much later period than " The Beggar's Opera," and a play which calls for far more sentiment and softness and gracefulness.

" The Duenna," it will be remembered, is a play purporting to deal with Spanish life; but Sheridan himself never visited Spain, and there is very little evidence in the play that he troubled himself at all to reproduce a Spanish atmosphere, and certainly his production—if one can judge from a few pictures of it that still survive—took no notice of the fact that the scenes were laid in Spain at all, either in scenery or costume. Mr. Sheringham, however, very rightly, I think, took advantage of a fact which Sheridan himself, following the fashion of his time, discounted.

His Spanish dancers' dresses, and to some extent the dresses of his principal characters, were founded upon the earlier pictures of Goya; they were softer and at the same time gayer than the contemporary English pictures of the same period. They helped to prove what a variety of effect can be obtained from the late eighteenth-century shapes and contour, and proved once again what a mistake it is to suppose that the decoration of an eighteenth-century play must necessarily be a repetition of what has been seen upon the stage over and over again.

To suggest that Sheringham is a mere follower of Lovat Fraser is a mistake, and a very careless and short-sighted mistake, though it is a mistake frequently made by critics of our productions.

Mr. Norman Wilkinson, again, who was responsible for two more of our productions, " The Rivals," and " Lionel and Clarissa," is yet another artist whose work is, no doubt, conducted upon the same theories which I have endeavoured to define, but who obtains entirely individual results. He also, as every good artist must do, studies first the character of the play with which he is called upon to deal, next studies a general colour-scheme in relation to his background, and then translates his design and effect into the idiom of the period with which he is dealing and the type of the comedy and characters who make up the play.

" The Rivals " is a comedy of manners, almost an actual reproduction of the manners of the times of Sheridan's youth. Here something realistic in the way of costume seems to be called for, and almost realistic is the treatment it receives at the hands of the artist. You feel that had you lived at that time, these were the people you would have met, and these were the dresses which they would be wearing. With just this difference, however, that just as conveniently they meet within the space of the two or three hours' traffic of the stage, so too, conveniently they happen to be wearing the very clothes that not only set off their characters, but blend harmoniously with each other and their sayings and doings.

In " Lionel and Clarissa " it is not quite the same thing. It is a period more remote, not only in time, but in actuality. They move to music— they dance their thoughts. So their costumes must be more imaginative, less actual. I do not know as he enters the room that one could ever have met that young fop in the flesh; surely his wig (" he could wait no longer for your curling irons ") is a little too high to be possible. Does it matter? When he sets himself a-jigging, his frills and furbelows and his rouged cheeks seem supremely right. It would be as wrong to doubt them as to inquire too curiously whether the two young ladies could have worn such daintiness unsullied, even through the very mild adventures of a day and an evening in a garden.

Here quite rightly Mr. Wilkinson allows himself a daring in the combination of colours which he would have been afraid of risking in Sheridan's comedy.

In the entertainment now being given at this theatre, as I write, you may see a group which at first sight would seem rudely to controvert all the canons I have put forward. It is in the last scene of a kaleidoscopic review; the review has some thirteen scenes and the dresses and scenery of them have been designed by four different artists—Phillippe Forbes-Robertson, Michael Sevier, James Whale and John Armstrong. There are ladies and gentlemen of the 1870's, sailors, landsmen and village maidens of 1750, music-hall singers, or fantasticated versions of them, from the odd period when Whistler and the youthful Sickert reigned over our imaginations, Elizabethan soldiers and our grandmothers of 1830, in a costume founded upon what they actually wore, but wildly supposing them to have taken to light ways and jigged it with the Ethiopian serenaders to the tune of "Buffalo Girls, will you come out to-night?" And here in this last scene they all meet and mix together—a band of amateur actors hungry and supping after their unaccustomed exertions. Is the effect wrong, and if not, why not?

It certainly pleases the eye of the audience, but what is my excuse after all my insistence upon supervision and the single responsibility of a designer? It is in that very word which I have just used and spelt, I hope, correctly— *kaleidoscopic*. It is an effect definitely intended to be syncopated—in accordance with the whole spirit of the scene; the mixture is the very essence of its rightness. The only thing here that could mar the design would be a single dress which was not amusing and characteristic. The scene *as a whole* can be left to look after itself.

But it is, as you will admit, a scene that cannot occur very often, and therefore can be legitimately claimed as the exception which proves the rule. Any other single scene in the whole entertainment would be ruined by the introduction of one dress which did not rightly belong to it.

As I have said, I purposely am not dealing in this chapter with plays of modern life, realistically treated; because I have nothing of general interest to say about them beyond this—that whatever the subject, high life, low life, middle life, there is always a picture to be presented and always a knowledge of character to be added to by a careful study of the dresses in which those characters appear. In the hey-day of the realistic school, of the brilliant series of comedies of contemporary life written by Shaw, Pinero, Henry Arthur Jones and Oscar Wilde, I always made this criticism to myself, and believe that it was justly made; that well and carefully as their production was handled, their effect would have been greater if an artist-designer of genius had been in control of their dressing.

As they were given, one had always the feeling that though the words were well and naturally spoken, the movements made with grace and naturalness, the appearance of the characters was far too often the appearance of dressmakers' models and tailors' dummies rather than real human beings. An old theatrical story will be remembered in this connection. A famous firm of dressmakers sent a message to a manager : " Please let some other actress play the part of ——, Miss —— does not suit our model costume." The story, far-fetched as it sounds, may very conceivably be founded upon fact.

Though I have taken trouble in this way over all my modern productions, I would modestly call attention to the remarkable series of the productions of Tchekhov's plays at the Barnes Theatre to point the moral of the advantage to the play of careful dressing.

And now I think I can return to and sum up these rules that I have laid down for my own guidance, and hope that they may be useful to other producers, though they are in all conscience simple and obvious enough.

1. Every play that is a consistent play, and every scene in an entertainment that is consistent in itself, should be designed with the costumes of the actors by one artist.

2. He should design them with due regard to the lighting, the characters of the persons concerned, and the style of the dialogue and the period in which it is spoken.

3. The personality of the artist is of more importance than his knowledge of detail, but a good deal of knowledge will do him no harm so long as he can forget it at the right moment.

COSTUME AT THE LYRIC THEATRE, HAMMERSMITH—II

By Amelia Defries and Maria Pitt-Chatham

Go through the Western world and see how, in the modern theatre, three influences are at work in all that pertains to stage costumes and settings. See how these influences are not only a new stimulus to the dressmakers but how they have actually, for mechanical reasons, made possible the whole Little Theatre movement, through Europe and America, giving new life to old plays, new style to young playwrights, opportunities for new artists who, thus enabled to express their personal taste, have transformed the taste of others until the effect they have had on daily life (outside the theatre) may be seen in private houses, in shops, in everyday clothes, even in our hair and our very faces; and the " commercial theatre," lagging behind, is doing to-day what they were doing ten years ago.

All this is the work, not of playwright or of actor, as such, but of the visual artist in the theatre.

Before the war three men stood at the head of the stream of thought and torrent of labour which has made this possible; they were Gordon Craig, Appia, and Stanislavski, each making his personal contribution and, as an American writer has said, " of them all the greatest original genius is that of an Englishman, Edward Gordon Craig, who has influenced the world."

By these three men and those who came after them the theatre has been transformed, until to-day you may see in the Vaudeville scrapped pieces of what these artists were doing before the war !

The style they have created is, in short, no longer confined to special audiences, it has reached the public in general; though this is not to say that the things now set before the public are such as these artists would have done if they themselves had received the commissions that went, for various reasons, to lesser men in commercial industries. Nevertheless, fresh air has blown over us and everything we use has become simpler in form, better in line, more natural and in better colour.

In a word, they started what is no less than the style of our own day; and for this reason, if for no other, they will go down in history, since by their fashions as much as by their actions do we know our ancestors; and it is largely by our style our descendants will know us.

In thinking of costume at the Lyric Theatre, Hammersmith, one must never forget its source, though where the Lyric differs from the pre-war pioneer theatres is that it has found a way to use art with a practical economy such as had never been known in our time; in saying this, of course, we take into consideration the change in the value of money and its altered purchasing power.

Mr. Playfair discovered how to get effects without costly materials and how to provide the illusion needed, without expensive scenery. Instead of banishing fine art as too luxurious, he called it in because it was so cheap! Art is economy, he discovered (did the world but know this, how beautiful might our surroundings become!). The artist is the best craftsman, the one who really knows his job, the one who understands how to create effects by subtle means, such as nature herself uses. The artist has by instinct and training, if he be an artist worthy of the name at all, a true sense of values; that is, of the relative value of one tone against another, of one material in juxtaposition to another; and he knows how to bring out this, and how to set back that, how to simplify, how to *use* materials. Wasteful, lavish methods are not those of the true artist, whose mental process is that of elimination and of selection. And so not only may costume be transformed, but people too; for if nature makes us, art refines us; and it is this sense of refinement of feeling that is the most lasting note in all the costumes at the Lyric Theatre. Good taste, in fact—so rare a treasure, on the stage and off it, that our eyes open wide with surprised delight whenever we do chance to see it.

The artist can really make a beautiful woman, invent one as it were, if he knows how to dress her, if he knows the character she ought to be, if he knows the materials and the hues she ought to wear, if he invents or discovers a " line " for her.

All the women in " The Beggar's Opera " looked beautiful, and, as for the bevy of girls that sailed on to the stage in " Polly," they were so entrancing that people held their breath at the sight of them. How was this effect obtained? By instinct and experience; such artists as Lovat Fraser or William Nicholson knew how to use a bit of velvet for a low tone here, a bit of satin for a high light there; to turn a piece of silk inside out for half tones; and, how to use the pure range of silks just where they were wanted in the picture, even as nature uses texture in flowers to get the lights and tones and the sensation needed for sheer beauty. The result of these costumes, in the proper setting, went a very long way to make the successes of the plays, for they not only provided a delight to the eye, as feasts of colour, arranged so that they appeared new and fresh, but they actually enhanced the beauty of the women and the looks of the men. Did not Edward Carpenter once say " to come near to understanding the use of materials is divine? "

That understanding has been a large part of the wisdom which has made the costumes at the Lyric Theatre what they are; for each material has its character, its personality, just as every pigment has, just as every flower has, only very few indeed are sensitive enough, few have trained their sense of perception enough, few have the eye or the hand to be able so to use materials as to seem "divine,"—capable of flooding the stage and the hearts of men and women with delight.

Before the war Granville Barker had worked with artists, with Norman Wilkinson, with Albert Rutherston, taking bits of Craig principle and seeing what they could make of it by a system of compromise to suit the financial position they were then in; that is to say, they took things as they found them, which Craig would not do, and they did not wait, as Craig did, for a dream to come true; they started where they were and used what came to hand. They, too, were, in their way, pioneers; they got away from the heavy late Victorian tradition, with its lavish expenditure. But they did not produce, and no one else has produced, the great art which might actually have come had Craig had his own way.

But they did something. They started. And their influence went far, even to Paris, where the Vieux Colombier was indebted to Norman Wilkinson. Then it was Mr. Barker who, when in New York, found out a young American student, Robert Edmund Jones, and gave him the chance to make the costumes for his first production, " The Dumb Man's Wife." So has English influence gone abroad in the U.S.A., for Jones is now one of their two leading artists in the theatre.

It is good to realise that in this art England has sent, and is sending out, the spirit of fine craft and of fine taste; even though she herself has learnt much from what Russia, Germany, France, and Italy have sent to her. Mr. Playfair came into the arena at a time when even funds such as had seemed small in the days of Barker's beginnings were not available. Where other men might have seen obstacles, he saw possibilities. He took an old theatre, given over to melodrama, and to beer-drinking, orange-eating audiences, next to a doss-house, hidden in a side street of a London terminus; " no one " ever went there, no one would ever come there, the ordinary manager would have thought; but because it had a style which he gave it, it actually set a fashion and drew " all London."

If famous artists could not be afforded, then why not give the young and the untried a chance? They are cheaper, naturally, at the start.

And an artist, if the right one be chosen, can create atmosphere out of next to nothing.

One is reminded of the story of Saint Teresa, who (to put a beautiful old legend into two words) determined to see a hospital put up in a city where the councillors thought it could not be done. They said to her, " There is no money," and she replied " Here are two pennies, and here is Teresa." The hospital was built and stands to this day.

In a word the management of the Lyric Theatre at Hammersmith had Faith, and by Faith may all things be accomplished.

A Paris art critic in London during the run of " The Way of the World " was roused to enthusiasm by its beauty, and said nothing in Paris could compare with it, the exquisite English of the play being, as it were, repeated in the costumes and scenery.

Similarly an American producer of intellectual and artistic works, when in London on a flying visit, spent his one night rushing from " The Beggar's Opera " to " Polly," because he had heard they were the most original productions here at the time.

The practical question arising in our mind is, how was this fame achieved, how did the management set to work?

They set to work with natural and cultivated taste and, trusting to rising talent rather than to famous names, they backed their own judgment, and gave to the youth they discovered the chance of its life. A definite " school " of the Art of the Theatre has resulted and has found its place even in Museum archives.

We live in an era when there are some signs at least of that Elizabethan spirit which goes by the name of "Merry England," and among the centres of this revival or rebirth stands the Lyric Theatre with its purely English outlook of jovial good humour and refinement of broad style. That is one of the secrets of the costumes as well as of the acting, its sometimes daring breadth without a trace of coarseness. All in the mood of pure sport, yet sensitive to human weaknesses !

The first play chosen for the transformed theatre was " Make Believe," by A. A. Milne, who was then " becoming known." These words help us to understand the gifts of this manager with the collector's *flair* for what will become valuable. What is becoming known, even what should become known, is his material, and he knows where to find what he wants; he has not only made a reputation, but he is a maker of reputations. It is in his own account of his first production at the Lyric that the name of Claude Lovat Fraser first crops up; and he set the style of the costumes at the Lyric Theatre. A free hand was given to Lovat Fraser, and "for the first time that extraordinary simplicity combined with what our grandfathers called elegance, for which he was famous, appeared on the English stage."

This elegant simplicity has been the " note " in the costumes and scenery of the Lyric Theatre ever since; and upon it grew up the " school " whose influence has now spread beyond its place of origin.

This style made it possible to re-interpret without too much expense the eighteenth century, and to make a stand for the purity of the English idiom.

The production of " La Serva Pedrona " decided the policy of the Lyric Theatre. The Management established the theory that the designs which dressed a play were equal in importance to the play itself, and that it was as necessary to discover the right artist as to settle on the right play.

Of course, there was nothing new in using an artist to design costumes and scenery. Irving had done it—had he not called into the theatre Madox Brown himself and others of the pre-Raphaelite Brotherhood? His Victorian methods were too costly for our day—besides, modern art has realised that realistic attention to minute and exact detail is not necessary to provide delight for the eye of the beholder. Lovat Fraser led the way to this realisation. Inexpensive methods, he proved, might hold as much elegance and charm as the past with its luxury had given. Necessity became the mother of experiment. And not only did he achieve his æsthetic aim, but he even designed scenery that was "mechanically ten times as efficient and financially several times as cheap."

It is not possible to divorce scenery from costume, and though we are here set down to write of costume only, we cannot resort to the surgical operation of cutting the parts from the whole.

First there is the play, then the play has to be dressed, afterwards the actors have to wear the costumes, move *in* the scenery and act the play. Writer, artist, and actor must be welded together so that unity and singleness of purpose appears as the result of their co-operation.

In the " Beggar's Opera " the Lyric Theatre achieved the unity which lies at the heart of perfection in art; moreover, by calling in at the same time Mr. Frederick Austin, the production was provided with a musician capable of raising the accompanying music to the height of the play, of the setting and of the acting. The unity was complete, and the play was an unforgettable event in the history of the English drama. But before the " Beggar's Opera," " As You Like It " was produced; departing from tradition, Lovat Fraser went direct to missals contemporary with the supposed period of the action of the play. What most people imagined to be cubistic was in reality faithfully transcribed from the fourteenth century !

We cannot ignore, from the craftsman's point of view, the materials used.

An understanding of how to select and handle material is a fundamental matter in all real art and any artist worthy of the name will either make his design suit his materials or select his materials to suit his design. To some artists this comes instinctively, but those who have it not must acquire it by technical training.

Lovat Fraser seems to have had—besides evident previous study—an instinct for it. He used, in this case, chiefly unbleached linen, all of it being dyed in the family bath. It is recorded that the reds and yellows were chiefly done with saffron, and that dyes at the time were still hard to get, but we are not told how the other colours were obtained. A knowledge of chemistry such as every painter should have, but seldom does have, must have sprung at his bidding from the previous studies of the designer.

In this production Lovat Fraser insisted on every actress doing away with her eyebrows, as he said that was the contemporary fashion. From this it may be seen that he ignored neither history nor detail in staging Shakespeare.

But in thinking of the Lyric Theatre we are almost obsessed by memories of " The Beggar's Opera," prepared and produced within five weeks ! Fraser was given a free hand with sole control over the designs for costumes and sets, and his work in " The Beggar's Opera " has become part of the history of English Art outside as well as inside the theatre; even the austere portals of the British Museum have opened to it. Its influence has gone far and wide—a whole generation of younger artists have grown up imbued with it—it has entered, in spirit, into dress-fashion and into house-decoration, into pottery, and many other forms of industrial design, posters not excluded.

The artist got rid of all that was unwieldy in tradition and obtained the spirit rather than the body of Hogarth and of Gay. No one has since done anything equal to his "Beggar's Opera" costumes, nor, indeed, has anyone connected with designing for this Theatre been able quite to "get away" from them. They have become a tradition, they have founded a definite "school," no one wants to forget them, they were such a delight that, in our time, at any rate, there is no need to get too far away from them—their aroma is still fresh and they stand as an impetus to the generation which came after their inventor.

What, actually, was their charm? It lay in the simple dignity of their proportion, and in the restrained and masterly use of colour. Broad passages of pure colour, fearlessly employed, coupled with broad caricature of the fashions of the period of the play.

Behind Lovat Fraser's simplicity there was a deep technical knowledge of art and its methods. And that, we think, is the reason those costumes made pictures which absolutely satisfied us.

We have said that he employed pure colour—yet, strictly speaking, though the result was that of clear purity, the colour was, of course, mixed to the shade needed, and so was never crude or hard, on the contrary; though dazzling at times, it was remarkable for softness and, therefore, for refinement in general tone.

While the "Beggar" was still running, Mr. Playfair undertook the production of "Polly" at another theatre, the experienced hand of Mr. William Nicholson being on this occasion employed.

The next play that matters to us was "The Way of the World," which its producer called "the greatest of all comedies of manners"; and for its costumes and scenery Doris Zinkeisen became responsible.

Influenced, as was only natural, by Lovat Fraser, Miss Zinkeisen stepped out on to ground of her own and her work was fresh and satisfying.

In "Midsummer Madness," by Clifford Bax, a new problem was solved by Mr. George Sheringham. The problem was to fill the stage and satisfy the eye with never more than four figures available with which to compose the variety needed in a stage picture. The play was modern, a fantasy in the mood of an earlier time. Basing his costume on the early Victorian tradition Mr. Sheringham invented a style, akin to that of previous Lyric Theatre productions in its cheerful ease and he set it against a garden blue and pink with English country flowers and green box hedge.

Mr. Sheringham's setting of "The Duenna" was charming. Like his predecessor he is entirely English in his outlook. And, in keeping with the Lyric "school," he managed in "The Duenna" to make several scenes out of one set with entire success.

He treated his subject in his own manner, modernising or re-interpreting the period to suit his fantasy, but keeping close to tradition in cut and character, working in with the English style of the play the Spanish influence of the *mise en scène*.

In "The Duenna," two chairs were the only furniture, so that the scene, by the manipulation of a few drops, could be completely changed in about four or five seconds.

In 1925 first " The Rivals " and then " Lionel and Clarissa " were staged, and Norman Wilkinson was entrusted with the costumes and scenery of both plays. He has a bright wit in his costumes, and upheld the tradition of a theatre where detail has been secondary to colour, and where spontaneous effects have been obtained with that appearance of a minimum of effort which is the mark of the master in art.

CLAUDE LOVAT FRASER.
"Beau Brummel."
For Blanchard Jerrold's "Beau Brummel."

PLATE LV

CLAUDE LOVAT FRASER
" Beau Brummel."
For Blanchard Jerrold's " Beau Brummel."

BLANCHARD JERROLD'S
"BEAU BRUMMELL."

DESIGN FOR A STAGE DRESS.
"BRUMMELL."

Chas. Ricketts. 30. Nov. 1920.

PLATE LVI

CLAUDE LOVAT FRASER
Costume Design.
For Marlowe's " Dr. Faustus."

MARLOWE'S "DOCTOR FAUSTUS."

DESIGN FOR A
STAGE DRESS.
"FAUST."

"*Miralda Clements*"

PLATE LVII

CLAUDE LOVAT FRASER
" Miralda Clements."
For Lord Dunsany's " If."

"IF" BY LORD DUNSANY.

DESIGN FOR A
STAGE DRESS
"MIRALDA CLEMENTS"

PLATE LVIII

CLAUDE LOVAT FRASER
" Lady Wishfort."
For Congreve's " The Way of the World."

THE WAY OF THE WORLD,
BY CONGREVE —

DESIGN FOR A
STAGE DRESS
LADY WISHFORT

PLATE LIX

WILLIAM NICHOLSON
" Mrs. Ducat."
For Gay's " Polly."
Reproduced by permission from the original at the Victoria and
Albert Museum

Mrs Ducat

PLATE LX

WILLIAM NICHOLSON
" Morano."
For Gay's " Polly."
Reproduced by permission from the original at the Victoria and
Albert Museum

Kerchief for head

Gold earrings

Grey tie wig

Gold Waist Coat

Buff Shirt

Indigo Velvet

Morano

WILLIAM NICHOLSON
Mrs. Diana Trapes
For Gay's "Polly"
Reproduced by permission from the original at the Victoria and
Albert Museum

PLATE LXI

WILLIAM NICHOLSON
" Mrs. Diana Trapes. '
For Gay's " Polly."
Reproduced by permission from the original at the Victoria and
Albert Museum

Jamaica Rum

Wine above Salt

gold brocade   Sass.

PLATE LXII

GEORGE SHERINGHAM
" Widow Pascal."
For Clifford Bax's " Midsummer Madness."

"Midsummer Madness"
by
CLIFFORD BAX

GEORGE SHERINGHAM

WIDOW PASCAL
(MISS TEMPEST)

PLATE LXIII

GEORGE SHERINGHAM
" The Duenna."
For Richard Brinsley Sheridan's " The Duenna."

GEORGE SHERINGHAM

THE DUENNA (first dress)
(ELSIE FRENCH)

PLATE LXIV

GEORGE SHERINGHAM
" Donna Clara."
For Richard Brinsley Sheridan's " The Duenna."

SHERIDAN'S
"THE DUENNA"

GEORGE SHERINGHAM

DONNA CLARA
(ISOBEL McLAREN)

PLATE LXV

GEORGE SHERINGHAM
" Pantaloon."
For Clifford Bax's " Midsummer Madness."

"Midsummer Madness"
by
Clifford Bax

Pantaloon
(Frederick Ranalow)

George Sheringham

PLATE LXVI

DORIS ZINKEISEN
" Mrs. Marwood."
For Congreve's " The Way of the World."

The Way of the World

Mrs Marwood

Zinkeisen

PLATE LXVII

DORIS ZINKEISEN
" Petulant."
For Congreve's " The Way of the World."

The Way of the World

Petulant

Zinkeisen

PLATE LXVIII

NORMAN WILKINSON
of Four Oaks.
" Jessamy."
For Isaac Bickerstaffe's Lionel and Clarissa."

JESSAMY

NORMAN WILKINSON
OF FOUR OAKS
1925

PLATE LXIX

NORMAN WILKINSON
of Four Oaks.
" Dorante."
For Molière's " The Would-be Gentleman."

DORANTE

SAX BLUE TAFETTA
COAT
ALMOND PINK
RIBBONS

OLD GOLD BROWN
FUR & LACE CUFF

IVORY TAFFETA
SHIRT & DRAWERS

OLD GOLD UNDER
SKIRT
WHITE
HAT
VER. PINK OSTRICH
PLUMES

NORMAN WILKINSON
1926

VERMILION PINK
STOCKINGS
WHITE SHOES

PLATE LXX

VICTOR HEMBROW
" Cyrano."
For Rostand's " Cyrano de Bergerac."

VICTOR HEMGROW

PLATE LXXI

VICTOR HEMBROW
" The Dancing Master."
For Goldsmith's " The Grumbler."

PLATE LXXII

JOHN ARMSTRONG
"Sailor."
For "Riverside Nights."
By A. P. Herbert and Nigel Playfair.

VI
REVUE

REVUE

By Charles B. Cochran

A comprehensive review of the costumier's department of modern theatrical decoration is a timely contribution to the bibliography of drama, since the last few years have witnessed a revolution in the art of costume as applied to *mise en scène*.

The old garish and often tasteless over-elaboration of decorative treatment, both of scene and costume design, which was only one of the absurdities of what we now call the pre-Robertsonian dramaturgy, quite naturally perished before the onslaughts of the later naturalistic tradition. A more staid and realistic literary drama was bound to affect the visual elements of production. The rococo and the emphatic in costume went the way of the rhetorical method of acting. The growing tendency towards simplicity, even towards mediocrity and drabness, was reflected in the robes of the Thespian. But as the drama is by its very nature—dramatic, so the theatre can never fulfil itself by holding the mirror up to the merely ordinary. The trend to naturalism, which cleared the scene of much that was distracting and ridiculous, was quickly destined itself to be replaced by a newer æsthetic in which beauty of line and colour, and richer harmonies of both than realistic latter-day costume could afford, were to have their honoured place.

To-day the pendulum is surely swinging back towards a more elaborate style of theatrical decoration, but with the greater elaboration are combined æsthetic consistency, a nicer regard for archæological and historical exactitude, and elements of stylisation ignored by the older school of decorators who specialised in the exaggeratedly picturesque.

I believe that the *mise en scène* of the future will avail itself increasingly of decorative art, particularly in regard to costume. After all, the dressing of a part and of a stage is one of the most important adjuncts of productional art. Costume can express the meaning, the mentality, and the dramatic significance of a given character. If desired, costume can heighten these or reduce them to a symbolical or abstract form. In such ways the costume designer can make manifest the intention of the dramatist, and prove a valuable ally to the producer.

The legitimate theatre still has a long way to go before it achieves the complete use of those means of greater expression which the art of the modern costumier has placed ready to its hands. It is when we turn to revue production that we see how powerful an aid costume can be to the theatre of the future. It would be difficult to over-emphasise the importance of the enormous impetus which had been given to the *décor* of the British theatre by the productions of revue during the last decade.

Throughout this century the revolt against decorative naturalism has been steadily developing in the theatre, but it was not until revue, in an essentially English form, was introduced to the British stage by me in the early days of the war that this revolt may be said to have expressed itself to any extent in the so-called commercial theatre. I have always regarded richness of colour and attractiveness of line as a vital necessity of the theatre as a whole. Thus in successive revue productions I sought to foster to the full the representative achievements of the best decorators of the English and foreign art worlds. In my spectacular revues from " The League of Notions," " Mayfair and Montmartre," " Fun of the Fayre," " London, Paris, and New York," and so on, right down to the recent productions " Still Dancing " and " On with the Dance " at the Pavilion, I have sought to give full rein to the skill or fantasy of the world's leading decorators, especially in regard to costume. My stage directors and myself have striven, by the employment of unusual materials and new devices of illumination, to show how the technique of the modern theatre can assist the designer in producing the maximum of effect, and so to make costume a more considerable element than ever before in theatrical art, in the widest conception of the term.

I venture to hope that my efforts in this direction have reinforced and complemented the remarkable achievements in this sphere which have had so considerable an influence in the decoration of the theatres of the world, thanks to my friend M. Serge Diaghileff, the creator and impresario of the Russian Ballet.

Revue, of course, offers very considerable opportunities for the development of the more spectacular aspects of *mise en scène*. But these need by no means be confined solely to that particular art-form. Musical comedy and light opera productions teem with possibilities for picturesque costume treatment, and although of late years great strides have been made in this direction, these possibilities have by no means yet been completely realised. I am often struck, for example, by incongruities between scene and costume, and would advance here a plea for the decoration of a given piece to be conceived as a whole. Revue can offer a variety of decorational techniques from scene to scene, but consistency throughout would seem to be demanded in the case of a musical comedy or operetta.

Grand opera production in this country has proved almost impossibly conservative, so far as the new theatrical art is concerned. Here surely is a field where the modern decorator can reap a rich harvest.

In my own musical productions, apart from revue, I have sought to avail myself of his aid—" Afgar " may be cited as one example. When we consider the legitimate stage, with the obvious exception of the conventional drawing-room play, or other realistic or pseudo-realistic dramas, the advisability of calling to the full upon the good offices of designers of the first class becomes even more apparent. For instance, my production of " Cyrano de Bergerac " was enormously enhanced in appeal, thanks to the decorative treatment which it received at the hands of Edmund Dulac. I think I can take credit to myself for being the first manager to enlist for the stage the services of this distinguished artist, who succeeded quite as notably in his designs for " Phi Phi " as in those which helped to make " Cyrano " one of the greatest artistic achievements of our post-war theatre.

Another eminent English decorator, who rightly claims a place of high honour in this volume, William Nicholson, is here represented only by theatrical designs from productions at the Lyric, Hammersmith, with which he has been associated. I do not think it is mere *parti pris* which makes me regard the work which this artist did in the Pavilion revues for the Hogarth Ballet and " The Tub " as of an altogether more highly imaginative order. Miss Doris Zinkeisen, whose " The Way of the World " costumes are justly represented in a work illustrative of the high achievements of the contemporary costume designer, has also been associated with my revues at the Pavilion and in the various cabaret spectacles that I have presented of late at the Trocadero. In dressing these last—I have been at as much pains as in preparing the costumes for a big spectacular revue such as " The Fun of the Fayre," and the success of these meal-time entertainments, which depend so much on the visual effect, serves to indicate the importance of costume in this new and popular type of amusement. Miss Zinkeisen's more recent work shows steadily increasing understanding and imagination.

I am glad to see Oliver Messel's masks exemplified in this volume, for, controversial as their use may be, I believe that the theatrical mask will command increasing attention in the theatre of the future. Once a common adjunct of the actor's equipment, the mask has now fallen to the estate of a mere curiosity. But in the hands of artists its reinstatement should not, given the proper conditions, be a matter of difficulty. That is why I take pride in having introduced Mr. Messel's masks to the theatrical public in my last revue.

Costume for me is one of the most provocative and interesting departments of theatrical experiment. So entertaining is it that I have allowed this attraction to overrule my former announced decision to give up revue production. Thanks in part to my interest in theatrical decoration, and to the co-operation of many of the world's leading artists, the London Pavilion has become a Mecca of stage *décor*, whither students from all parts of the world repair in search of inspiration and example. The Venetian scene from " The Fun of the Fayre " created by Jean Gabrielle Domergue has been copied all over the world. André Derain has done nothing more beautiful than his *Gigue* mountings, which formed a part of Cochran's Revue, 1926. Gustave Bacarisas performed a miracle of costuming in his treatment of the Charles X period in my revival of the " Coppelia " ballet at the Trocadero.

The influence of colour, design, light, and beauty in all its manifestations as applied in any particular department of the theatre, will unfailingly redound to the advantage of the theatre as a whole and have a very definite bearing on the art of the theatre which, it appears, is now in course of rebirth throughout the world. Never was so much experimental work being done and, what is more important, never did experiment attract so large a share of the attention alike of the people of the theatre and of theatre-goers. From my own experience, resulting from the efforts which I have myself made in London, I should unhesitatingly predict a place of high honour in the theatrical comity of the future for the imaginative costume designer.

PLATE LXXIII

DORIS ZINKEISEN
" Clown's Dress."
For one of Mr. C. B. Cochran's Cabaret Shows.

PLATE LXXIV

GLADYS SPENCER CURLING
" Star."

PLATE LXXV

GLADYS SPENCER CURLING
" Orchid."

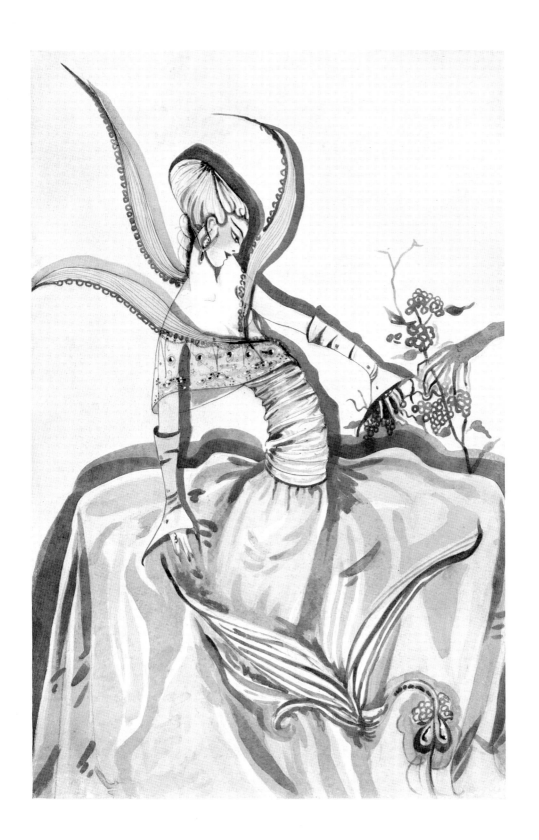

PLATE LXXVI

PAUL ROTHA
" Le Capitaine."

OLIVER MESSEL

PLATE LXXVII

OLIVER MESSEL
" Negro Hyacinth " (Mask).

PLATE LXXVIII

OLIVER MESSEL
" Winged Icarus " (Mask).
By kind permission of Glyn Philpot, Esq., R.A.

PLATE LXXIX

OLIVER MESSEL
" Hawaiian Mask."
Reproduced by permission of Fenwick Cutting, Esq.

PLATE LXXX.

OLIVER MESSEL.

PLATE LXXX

OLIVER MESSEL
" Jehanne " (Mediæval Mask).

VII
COSTUME IN OPERA

P

COSTUME IN OPERA

By Marguerite d'Alvarez.

Costume in Opera !—how poor the reality !—how wonderful the seldom-met ideal—the costume that truly expresses the spirit, the personality of the character portrayed !

This, when it can be achieved, is an inspiration in itself and brings one at once into contact and mental sympathy with the rôle one is singing. At once, the singer walks differently, thinks differently, feels differently. He or she has more courage, for costume is a spiritual armour. It hides the singer from the world and reveals only the personality of the part.

For this reason, there should be at least six dress rehearsals of every opera, and the actors should be obliged to rehearse in their costumes. Then they would lose all self-consciousness, and there would be no bad actors, except those with no particle of emotion, for they would find gestures and drama come to them spontaneously through their costume. One famous tenor I knew, used actually to live in his, but this, for those with imagination, is carrying the idea a little far !

Artists, alas ! are seldom artists in everything, or they would realise instinctively the costume that each part demands, and we should not so often be faced by the sad spectacle of a singer singing divinely a heroic rôle, in a costume that recalls only the hero of suburban pantomime.

Hergesheimer says of one of his characters—a dancer—that the whole history of Spain was in the movement of her hips.

As much can be expressed by the folds of a singer's gown.

I must confess I find it difficult to take seriously any artist who fails to realise the importance of costume in the giving-of-life to a visionary figure, that is the creation of an operatic rôle.

To the artist himself colour alone is—or ought to be—a vital help to interpretation. It can set the key-note of his emotional mood.

99

When I see a glorious tone of orange, for instance, everything is bathed in orange, becomes warmed and vivified, like a wonderful persimmon, kissed by the rays of the sun. And the orange and purple sunsets of Africa have been responsible for the creation of many of my costumes.

Beautiful materials—silks and brocatelles—can be a help, too, to inspiration. In my own home, I have coffers filled with marvellous old shawls and tissues, and even when practising I drape myself in these and hold them up and their supple beauty helps to give me a sense of the proportion of the phrases that could never be taught—just as the distances that separate the mountain peaks have been a constant inspiration to me in the architecture of the pauses in the phrasing of my songs.

On the public, too, how great is the effect ! The judgment of the ear is less critical when the eye has been seduced, and a second-rate singer can electrify, and almost satisfy, through a beautiful and inspiring costume. The entire spirit of an opera can be expressed or nullified by the costumes worn, and the emotional atmosphere of a scene created by the right use of colour in the grouping and truth to detail in the designs. This was well understood in the little theatre in Rouen where I made my first appearances. There the costumes, though most modest in fabric, often only of the humblest muslin and sateen—were painted by hand to simulate the old silks and brocatelles that the operas demanded and our company was inspected like a stud of race-horses before any member was allowed to set foot upon the stage.

So much importance was attached to this question that though I was then earning barely enough for food, I was forced by my contract to spend upon costumes in advance, one thousand pounds, that it took me five years to repay.

To-day, it seems that all beautiful things have to be taught, so each opera house should have a " period " director, who would be responsible for every detail of dress and *décor*, in order that all might be welded into a harmonious whole. He would see that the true atmosphere of each opera was created and the individuality of each character expressed through the medium of costume.

Carmen herself would be the spirit of Spain incarnate—a creature of curves and femininity, draped in silks and fringes that almost conceal the body she is in love with as she dances. So little is this conception understood to-day, that when I came out in real Spanish costumes worn by my great-grandmother, a storm of consternation was aroused and I received indignant letters asking where I had conceived the crazy idea of Spanish girls wearing long frilled skirts ! Delilah's costume, in contrast, should be a thing of jewels and the flesh, Pagan, Byzantine, conjuring up an orgy of colour and sound.

And as in the opera house, so on the concert platform, costume should help to build up the atmosphere of the song. Once, when I was singing in Australia, the greater part of the programme being Spanish, I was wearing a dress of flaming orange fringes with coral combs and jewels. Towards the end I was to sing the " Agnus Dei " and I had to crave the forgiveness of my audience and retire to the green-room, remove the combs and ear-rings and conceal the fringes under a shawl of plain gold tissue, before I could begin that uplifting aria, that needs no physical adornment, but only simplicity of the soul.

If this ideal could be better understood ! We have suffered too long from the spangled robes of *prime donne* and the costumes of tradition, worn by a hundred Siegfrieds, discarded by a thousand Fausts. We must have imagina-tion—poetry—symbolism in the costume of the future, to bring inspiration to the artist and understanding to the crowd. And this must apply too, to scenic design and production. All must work together to serve one end—the interpretation of the composer's message. Then we shall have harmony and a unity of Beauty—a perfect expression of artistic Truth.

VIII
COSTUME FOR BALLET

COSTUME FOR BALLET

By Cyril W. Beaumont

With illustrations by Randolph Schwabe

The origin of ballet is essentially aristocratic. It was the direct outcome of the elaborate court festivals which came into vogue at the close of the fifteenth century. The first recorded was the splendid entertainment held at Tortona in 1489, on the occasion of the marriage of Galeazzo, Duke of Milan, with Isabel of Arragon. Devised by Bergonzio di Botta, it took the form of a great feast at which each dish was presented with an appropriate dance. This event became famous throughout Europe so that every petty court aspired to possess its own ballet.

The new fashion found a warm patron in Catherine de Medici, who introduced it to the court of France as a diversion for her son Henry III, while she retained a firm grasp of the government. The greatest of such spectacles was that produced by Balthasar de Beaujoyeulx, called Baltazarini, on October 15, 1581: the " Balet Comique de la Royne " which celebrated the betrothal of the Duc de Joyeuse and Mademoiselle de Vaudemont, the Queen's sister. Baltazarini published his account of the ballet in a costly volume dated 1582, from which the following descriptions of certain of the costumes are taken.

" Circe the enchantress was in a robe of gold tissue, of two colours, covered with little puffs of silk threaded with gold and overlaid with great silken veils threaded with silver. The ornaments on her head, and about her neck and arms, were marvellously enriched with precious stones and priceless pearls. In her hand she held a golden wand, five feet in length, just as legendary Circe used, to touch men in order to change them into animals or inanimate things."

" The Naiads were clothed in silver tissue covered with silver and crimson veils which billowed about the hips and all round the body, and everywhere at the ends there were little puffs of crimson silk, threaded with gold, which added grace to the costume. Their leaders were adorned with little triangles enriched with diamonds, rubies, pearls, and other exquisite and precious stones. Their necks and arms were covered with necklaces, collarets, and bracelets, and all their clothing was covered with stones which shone and glittered as you see the stars appear at night in the blue vault of heaven. This adornment has been acclaimed to be the most superb, rich and pompous vestment ever seen in a masquerade."

In England, the ballet found expression in masques, of which the most famous were those by Ben Jonson. The decoration of the majority of his masques was entrusted to Inigo Jones. That he devoted considerable thought to his conceptions will be apparent from the following descriptions taken from Jonson's " The Masque of Blackness," given before the Court at Whitehall on Twelfth Night, 1605–6.

" Oceanus presented in a human form, the colour of his flesh blue, and shadowed with a robe of sea-green; his head grey, and horned, as he is described by the ancients; his beard of the like mixed colour; he was gyrlanded with alga, or sea-grass; and in his hand a trident."

" Splendor, in a robe of flame colour, naked breasted, her bright hair loose flowing; she was drawn in a circle of clouds, her face and body breaking through; and in her hand a branch with two roses, a white and a red."

" Germinatio, in green, with a zone of gold about her waist, crowned with myrtle, her hair likewise flowing, but not of so bright a colour; in her hand a branch of myrtle. Her socks of green and gold."

" Laetitia, in a vesture of divers colours, and all sorts of flowers embroidered thereon; her socks so fitted. A garland of flowers in her hand; her eyes turning up and smiling; her hair flowing, and stuck with flowers."

Jones also designed the scenery and costumes for many of the masques and entertainments written by Carew, Cartwright, Chapman, Daniel, D'avenant, Fletcher, Heywood, Shirley, and Townshend. Sir William D'avenant describes several of Jones's costumes for his masque " Britannia Triumphans " (published 1637), presented before the Court at Whitehall on the Sunday after Twelfth Night, 1637. Two examples must suffice :

" From several parts of the scene came Action and Imposture. Action a young man in a rich habit down to his knees with a large guard[1] of purple about the skirt wherein was written with silver letters MEDIO TUTISSIMA, on his head a garland of laurel, and in one hand a branch of willow. Imposture in a coat with hanging sleeves and great skirts, little breeches, a high-crowned hat, one side pinned up, a little ruff, and a formal beard and an angling rod in his hand with a fish at the hook, with a bag and horn at his girdle."

[1] An ornamental hem, lace or border.

DANCERS OF THE *GRAND BALLET*
After a design in the Louvre

Thus the ballet originated in Italy, was developed in France, to inspire the English masque, which in turn influenced the later French opera-ballets which were the foundation of the modern ballet.

In France, from 1611 to 1650, ballets were the almost inseparable accompaniment of all state ceremonies. Among those of particular interest were " La Douairière de Billebahaut " (1626), " Les Fées des Fôrets de Saint-Germain " (1626), and " Le Château de Bicêtre " (1632). The majority of these ballets contained a large element of buffoonery and the grotesque, which spirit was reflected in the costumes. They were invested with a primitive symbolism. In the " Entrée des couppetestes " in " Les Fées des Fôrets de Saint Germain," the dancers, armed with sword, club, or axe, wore false arms and heads, made of cardboard, which were struck off during the ballet. In the " Entrée de l'Hoste, de l'Hostesse et leur Valet " in the " Château de Bicêtre," the host, dressed in an exaggerated version of the costume of an innkeeper of the period, carried in one hand a cup and in the other a tankard, and wore a head-dress in the form of a wicker covering for a wine bottle. The coiners in the " Entrée des Faux Monnayeurs," which occurred in the same ballet, each wore a broad-brimmed hat with the crown banded with coins, and a jacket and breeches divided into squares, each enclosing a money token.

The noblemen taking part in these ballets spent immense sums on their costumes, regardless of the simplicity of the part which might be allotted to them; for example, a beggar would be dressed in torn clothes but made of the finest materials. The musicians who played the music for the ballets always had special dresses, irrespective of whether they appeared in the *entrées* or remained on their platforms. The accounts for the " Fées des Fôrets de Saint-Germain " include :

168 ells of crimson taffeta for 24 special costumes for the 24 Violinists of the King	672 livres of Tours
48 ells of crimson buckram to stiffen the said costumes	28 „ „ „
360 ells of gold and silver lace for the said costumes	73 „ „ „
24 ells of gold braid	3 „ 12 sols
16 ounces of crimson silk for sewing the said costumes	14 „ 8 „

Whether the theme of a ballet was noble or burlesque, mythological or romantic, allegorical or realistic, and whether it was explained by words recited or sung, or by a series of pictures, the sole purpose of the different *entrées* was to provide a suitable excuse for the entry of dancers, wearing black or gold masks, and diadems adorned with tinselled aigrettes and plumes, who danced the figures of the concluding *Grand Ballet*. These dancers were dressed alike in rich costumes, the men usually in a tight-fitting jacket with short scalloped skirts of rich material which revealed the bare knee, the feet being incased in buskins reaching to the calf. The *Grand*

Ballet was sometimes danced by ladies and sometimes by noblemen. But in the ballets in which the king and his courtiers appeared, no woman, of whatever rank, took part.

Under Louis XIV, ballet made great progress, the grotesque and coarse side of the old productions gave place to a noble and dignified style due to the King's refined taste and the excellent artists he selected for the decoration of his ballets. At first, the personnel consisted of men alone, the female characters being taken by youths of feminine build whose faces were concealed by masks, then a fixed part of the dancer's costume.

In 1681, a ballet was given at Saint-Germain entitled " Le Triomphe de l'Amour," when the composer, Lully, introduced female dancers for the first time. The ladies of the Court took part in this piece, the Princess de Conti and Mlle de Nantes being among the first *danseuses*. The men were costumed in the recognised dress for dancers in the noble or serious style. Broadly considered, it was the dress of a Roman officer seen through seventeenth-century eyes. It consisted of a tight-fitting body like a Roman cuirass carried out in material, with short sleeves fringed with lace. The base of the body widened into a short pleated skirt, over which depended strips of material like the metal-faced straps that hung from the waist of the Roman warrior. This skirt was called a *tonnelet*. The head-dress was a diadem or helmet crested with plumes and perched on a high wig. The knees were left bare and the feet were shod with buskins reaching to the calf. The ladies wore the tight bodice and hooped skirt for the serious dance.

Perhaps the most famous costume designer at this period was Jean Berain, who was born near Bar-le-Duc about 1638. He came to Paris in 1659 where he worked as an engraver. In 1671 he was employed by the King and le Brun in the reproduction of ornaments executed in the Gallery of Apollo under the direction of the First Painter. Soon afterwards he gave up engraving and became a designer, his fertile imagination producing innumerable designs for embroidery, tapestry, wood carvings, and the decoration of war vessels. In 1675 he became *Dessinateur de la Chambre et du Cabinet du Roi*, and became responsible for the design of

COSTUME DESIGN FOR A GROTESQUE
DANCER (17TH CENTURY)
After Berain

all costumes and properties required in connection with the festivals and entertainments given by the King. The costumes of Berain are remarkable for their beauty of design, their graceful symbolism, their restraint and elegant artistry.

A dancer representing Endymion is dressed in a tight-fitting jacket with short sleeves, puffed with lace, and pointed tails falling over a short pleated skirt. He wears a diadem crested with plumes, and shoes and stockings of the period. In one hand he bears a short spear.

An Enchanter wears a long embroidered jacket with a fringed edge reaching to the knee, his waist is girt with a fringed sash, his feet are shod with buskins reaching to the knee. Over his jacket falls a fringed mantle with short and wide sleeves. On his head is a round hat crested with plumes, and in one hand he holds a slender wand.

A Bacchante has a short-sleeved tunic, open at the neck, bound at the waist with a garland of flowers and then widening into a short skirt. Over the right shoulder is a garland of flowers. The head-dress is composed of flowers built up in the form of a crown from which escape her flowing tresses. Her feet are shod in buskins and she carries a tambourine.

As an example of Berain's work in the grotesque manner, note the costume for a Cobbler. The dancer wears a plum-coloured jacket and breeches, pale blue stockings and brown leather shoes. Vari-coloured shoes are hung round his shoulders and chest. Two ragged leather aprons are tied about his waist. The head-dress is composed of soles and strips of leather, and two awls. His mask has a pointed nose and chin. In one hand he carries a knife and in the other a leather strap.

In 1704, Jean Berain was succeeded by his son who bore the same name. Père Menestrier, in his book " Des Ballets Anciens et Modernes," published in 1681, and dealing in part with the ballets of Louis XIV, lays down four conditions regarding costumes for ballet. " The first condition is that the costume should be appropriate to the subject and, if the personages be historical, one should keep as far as possible to the costume of their period. That of the ancient Romans is the most dignified of all, and there is not one that allows the leg more freedom. It is composed of a cuirass with its *lambrequins*. A short mantle accompanies it reaching half-way down the arms, below which is a pleated silken garment which forms the surcoat. The helmet with an aigrette and plumes is the head-dress which should accompany this dress and, when the dancers represent victorious troops, they must wear wreaths of laurels. The same rule applies to foreign nations. The Greeks have round caps with a quantity of plumes. The head-dress of the Persians is almost similar. The Moors have short and curly hair, their faces and hands black; they wear no hats, unless they be given fillets sewn with pearls in the form of a diadem. They should wear ear-rings. Turks and Saracens should be garbed in dolmans and wear turbans with aigrettes. American Indians wear caps with vari-coloured feathers, loin-cloths of the

COSTUME DESIGN FOR A TRITON (17th CENTURY)
After a drawing in the Archives of the Opéra, Paris

III

same kind to cover their nakedness, and necklaces of the same feathers of which they carry a bunch in each hand when dancing. Japanese wear large tufts of hair bound at the back . . .

" The second condition is that the costumes should be greatly varied and, if possible, the same kind of dress should not appear twice, or at least the *entrées* should be so devised that there is a long interval between those that are alike. The colour can be changed if it be not possible to make any other difference, as sometimes occurs in historical ballets when all the persons are of the same race and nearly the same station . . .

" The third condition is that uniformity should be maintained as far as possible in the *entrées*, that is to say, all those taking part in them should be dressed in the same colour and style if the subject permit.

" The fourth condition is that the costume shall not be cumbersome and shall leave the legs and body quite free to dance. The women's costumes are the least suitable because they must be long.

" If anything be put into the hands of the dancers it should serve for some action. Such as a hammer and trowel with which to imitate building, a sword to mimic fighting; Rivers pour water out of their urns, Zephyrs make a breeze with bunches of plumes and the Cyclops strike on an anvil."

As Menestrier declares, "the greatest difficulty lies in finding costumes appropriate to those imaginary persons and mythical beings whom we represent in human guise." The author then gives general directions for the costuming of familiar characters in ballets.

"The costume of Spring should be green sprinkled with flowers, and a garland of roses. Winter should be dressed in white with a long beard, a furred costume and appear sluggish in his movements. The dress of Summer should be isabel colour, which is that of the harvest, she must wear a crown of ears of corn on her head and carry a scythe. That of Autumn should be olive colour or that of dead leaves, with a cornucopia full of fruit, and a garland of vine leaves.

"Winds should be dressed in feathers on account of their lightness, the Sun in cloth of gold with a gilt headdress, the Moon in cloth of silver; both wear a mask, one with golden rays, the other with silver.

COSTUME DESIGN FOR *GEOMETRY*
(17th CENTURY)
After a drawing in the Archives of the Opéra, Paris

112

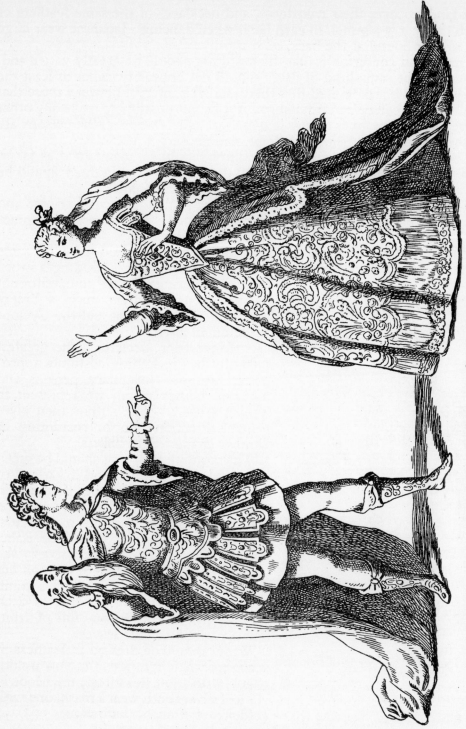

M. THEVENARD AND MLLE. LEMAURE RESPECTIVELY AS *LÉANDRE* (DISGUISED AS *SCAMANDRE* AND *CALLIRÉE* (1726).
After the drawing in the Archives of the Opéra, Paris

R   113

"Time should be dressed in four colours denoting the four seasons. For head-dress, he should wear a clock-face marking the hours, wings on his back and head, an hour-glass in one hand and a scythe in the other. Night should be dressed in black powdered with stars, and wear a crescent moon on her head. Cupid should be dressed in rose-coloured material, covered with flaming hearts, his eyes bandaged, a bow in his hand and a quiver on his back. Hate, on the contrary, should wear a fire-coloured dress and carry a dagger in one hand and poison in the other, or a smoking torch of black wax. The costume should be black because this passion is not free from sadness. Envy should wear a yellow costume dotted with open eyes. Poverty is recognised by a torn dress from which hang parti-coloured rags."

The Arts and Sciences were represented by working designs of the instruments and signs associated with them into the usual jacket and breeches in the case of a male dancer, or tight bodice and skirt in the case of a female dancer.

Tritons were represented with short, tight-fitting tunics and breeches, covered with silver cloth cut into scallops to suggest scales; the head-dress was formed of shells, the knees were each covered with a mask of a dolphin's head, and frequently the dancer danced holding a garland of material coloured and cut to represent seaweed and shells.

The most important feature of the dancer's costume, however, was the mask. Those of the Tritons were green and silver, those of the Demons red and silver, those of the Fauns blackish-brown, while those of the Winds had puffed-out cheeks.

The costumes of the dancers of Louis XV did not differ greatly from those of the previous reign. The men who executed the serious dance wore the plumed helmet and cuirass-shaped body as before, except that the latter was longer while the skirt was shorter, oval, of great width and so hooped that it projected to a considerable distance beyond the hips. The sleeves reached to the wrists and were puffed from the shoulder to the elbow. The buskins gave place to the shoes and stockings of the period. The dress of the *danseuses* consisted of a tight-fitting bodice and hooped, paniered skirt, adorned with ruchings of various materials, generally lace and feathers. The sleeves were puffed. The skirt followed the course of fashion in that it passed from a round to an oval shape, and then grew larger and flatter until the advent of the French Revolution. The perukes and costumes were in general much more exaggerated than those worn in the time of Louis XIV; on the other hand, the decoration of the costume, in which allegory and symbolism played their accustomed part, was more artistic and subdued.

At least three notable attempts at the reform of the dancer's costume took place in this reign. In 1726, Camargo made her first appearance. She is credited with the introduction in 1730 of the *entrechat*.[1] In order to gain the

---

[1] It must be stated that some form of *entrechat* was known before Camargo's time. Both Caroso (1581) and Feuillet (1701) describe a step corresponding to it. The *entrechat* was certainly executed by men long before 1726, but there are good grounds for believing Carmargo to have been the first *danseuse* to execute it.

M. VESTRIS AS *PLEASURE* (18th CENTURY)
After the design in the Archives of the Opéra, Paris

115

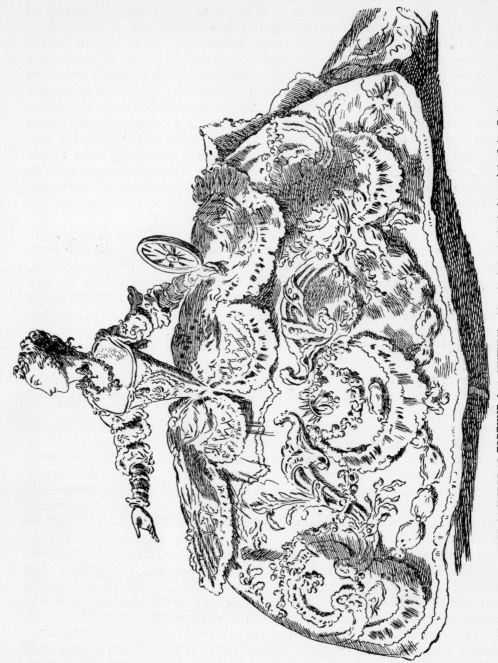

MLLE. LAGUERRE AS *FORTUNE* (18th CENTURY). After the design in the Archives of the Opéra, Paris

greater freedom in her legs required for the execution of this step, she caused her dress to be shortened by several inches, thus permitting the calf to be seen. But Camargo had the forethought to wear a small pair of close-fitting knickers while executing her new *temps d'elevation*. It is almost certain that this garment was the origin of the later *maillot* or tights, in which case it is no exaggeration to assert that the evolution of this intimate article of dress permitted as great a change in the art of dancing as did the invention of gunpowder on warfare. That Camargo's precaution was justified is proved by the mishap that occurred a little later to a young *danseuse* called Mariette, who, while springing in the air during the execution of a *pas*, caught her dress on a piece of scenery so that her petticoats were raised in full view of the audience with the most embarrassing results to the wearer. Soon afterwards, the police authorities issued an order that all actresses must wear the garment in question before appearing on the stage.

In 1734, the famous Marie Sallé accomplished a great step in the reformation of costume when she danced at London, on February 14, in " Pygmalion," a ballet of her own composition, and appeared " without paniers, petticoat, and bodice, her hair loose and without any ornament on her head; she was dressed only in a single muslin robe which was draped about her in the manner of a Greek statue."

In 1760, the celebrated *maître de ballet*, Jean Georges Noverre published his famous " Lettres sur la Danse et sur les Ballets." He condemned the dancer's costume in general and masks in particular. It is of interest to cite some passages from his book since no work, before or since, has produced so incalculably great an influence for good in the manner of ballet presentation.

" Let us pass to costume; its variety and accuracy are as rare as in music, in ballets and simple dancing. Obstinacy in adhering to out-worn traditions is the same in every part of opera, it is the monarch of all it surveys. Greek, Roman, Shepherd, Hunter, Warrior, Faun, Forester, Games, Pleasures, Laughs, Tritons, Winds, Fires, Dreams, High Priests, Celebrants—all these characters are cut to the same pattern and differ only in the colour and ornaments with which a desire for ostentatious display rather than good taste has caused them to be bespattered at caprice. Tinsel glitters everywhere; Peasant, Sailor, Hero—all are covered alike. The more a costume is decorated with gew-gaws, spangles, gauze and net, the greater the admiration it procures the ignorant spectator."

" I would do away with those *tonnelets* which in certain dancing positions transport, as it were, the hip to the shoulder and conceal all the contours of the body. I would banish all uniformity in costume, an indifferent, ungraceful device which owes its origin to lack of taste. I should prefer light and simple draperies of contrasting colours worn in such a manner as to reveal the dancer's figure. . . . . I desire beautiful folds, fine masses with the ends fluttering and producing ever-changing forms as the dance

117

becomes more and more animated; everything should convey a sense of filminess."

" I would reduce by three-quarters the ridiculous *paniers* of our *danseuses*, they are equally opposed to the freedom, speed, prompt and lively action of the dance. Again they deprive the figure of the elegance and correct proportions which it should have; they lessen the charms of the arms; they impede and trouble the *danseuse* to such a degree that the movements of her *panier* generally takes up far more of her attention than that of her arms and legs."

" Physiognomy, then, is that part of us most necessary to expression; well, why conceal it on the stage by a mask and prefer a clumsy art to beautiful nature? How can the dancer paint if he be deprived of his most essential colours? How can he transfer to the breast of the spectator the passions which consume his own, if he himself remove the means and cover his face with a piece of cardboard which ever appears sad and uniform, cold and motionless? "

" Can the passions be revealed and break through the screen which the dancer places between the spectator and himself? Can he make a single one of those artificial faces express the innumerable characteristics of the different passions? Will it be possible for him to change the form which the mould has given to the mask? Because a mask of whatever kind is either cold or pleasing, serious or comic, sad or grotesque. The modeller affords it but one permanent and unvarying character."

The mask was abolished in 1772 as the result of an incident during a revival of Rameau's opera, " Castor et Pollux." Gaetan Vestris, as usual, should have danced the *entrée* of Apollo in the fifth act. As this character he appeared in an enormous black peruke, a mask, and wore on his breast a large sun of gilded copper. But on this occasion Vestris was unable to appear and his part was allotted to Maximilien Gardel, a well-known dancer of the period and pupil of Noverre, who consented to appear provided that he was permitted to discard the wig and mask. The public was pleased and henceforth the solo dancers discarded the mask. It was, however, worn for some time longer by the *corps de ballet* for the representation of Shades, Winds, and Furies. Even as late as 1785 the Winds wore the usual mask with puffed out cheeks, but no longer carried the symbolic pair of bellows.

The most important designers of costumes during the reign of Louis XV were J. A. Meissonier (1736), A. S. Slodtz (1750), P. A. Slodtz (1754), R. M. Slodtz (1758), D. F. Slodtz (1764), Eisen and Boquet (*circa* 1762), Challes (1776), and Paris (1786). Boucher and Gillot also devised many dresses for ballets.

The shortening of the dress and the occasional use of a transparent material in its construction, led to the introduction of the *maillot* or tights, which are a combination of long stockings and close-fitting knickers. The introduction of tights is generally ascribed to Maillot, a costumier of the

Paris Opéra at the beginning of the century. But the use of tights was certainly known in the time of Guimard, who retired in 1790. There is also mention of this article of dress in the memoirs of the actor, Larrive. Again, the transparent dress worn by the *Merveilleuses* must have necessitated the use of a similar garment.

The French Revolution exerted a beneficial effect on the subject of stage costume. The fashion for light dresses modelled on the classic tunics and robes of the ancient Greek and Roman republics became transferred to the theatre. Certain prints of Maria Medina Vigano, a celebrated dancer of

DANCERS' COSTUMES OF 1820 AFTER BLASIS (CARLO) *TRAITÉ ELÉMENTAIRE, THÉORIQUE ET PRATIQUE DE L' ART DE LA DANSE.* Fig. 1. *DANSEUR SERIEUX.* Fig. 2. *DANSEUR DEMI-CARACTÈRE.* Fig. 3. *DANSEUR COMIQUE.*

this period, and the engravings which accompany the " Traité Elémentaire, Théorique et Pratique de l'Art de la Danse," of Carlo Blasis (Milan, 1820), afford an excellent idea of the costumes worn in the early years of the century. The male dancer in the serious style wore a Greek *chiton* of light material, his legs were bare and his feet shod in sandals strapped round the ankle and base of the calf. The *danseuse* was dressed in a filmy robe ending midway between the ankle and calf, the feet were encased in similar sandals. The costumes for dancers in the *demi-caractère* and *caractère* style are shown in the accompanying designs.

During the Restoration, the chaste Vicomte Sosthènes de la Rochefoucauld, Superintendent of the Royal Theatres, caused the dancers' skirts to be lengthened and ordered them to wear long pantaloons reaching below the skirt in place of tights. Happily this ridiculous concession to modesty did not long endure.

About 1832, the great Romantic period, the skirt of muslin or tarlatan came into being. It is regarded as the design of the painter Lamy for Taglioni's

MARIE TAGLIONI as *LA SYLPHIDE* (1832)

120

costume as the Sylphide in " La Sylphide." The bodice was tight-fitting, leaving the neck and shoulders bare, the sleeves were wide and very short, the skirt was bell-shaped and ended half-way between the ankle and the knee. Tights were worn and shoes were fashioned of leather soles with satin uppers. Taglioni danced *sur la pointe*, but the toe of her shoe was unblocked, being merely stiffened by darning with wool.

By 1840, the sleeves became shoulder straps which in later years were adorned with flares of muslin; the skirt was shorter and fuller, being stuffed with additional petticoats of tarlatan, and was shaped like a lamp-shade. Dancing *sur les pointes* became general and the shoe was blocked to give additional support to the toes, but it is difficult to ascertain precisely when this innovation was introduced. The muslin skirt, variously adorned with flowers, was now the fixed costume, one might say, uniform of the dancer. The costume of the male dancer was generally tight breeches ending above the knee, and a short jacket over a shirt open at the neck; in the case of the romantic ballets so common at this period, it consisted of parti-coloured *maillot*, a close-fitting doublet with puffed sleeves, and a velvet cap with a plume.

Towards the close of the century the technique of dancing was developed to its utmost limits in Russia, under the teaching of Marius Petipa. The complicated steps demanded more and more freedom for the legs and the dancer's skirt become shorter and shorter until it resembled a powder-puff. The basis of all costumes was the ballet skirt, pink tights and rose-coloured ballet shoes. If the dancer was intended to represent a Spaniard, the bodice was yellow and adorned with red ribbon, the skirt black. If the personage was Greek, a Greek key pattern was added to the edge of the skirt; if Egyptian, a lotus flower design was introduced; if a German peasant, the costume consisted of a dark velvet bodice, a small silk apron, and a few bands of red ribbon sewn to the edge of the skirt; if Hungarian, a few pieces of gold or silver braid were stitched horizontally across the bodice in hussar fashion, while the edges of the sleeves were tipped with fur. The dancer's *coiffure* followed the prevailing fashion, whatever character she interpreted, and it was generally ornamented with a diamond crescent or tiara. Balletomanes saw nothing incongruous in this, or nothing strange in that a dancer playing the part of a humble slave or simple peasant should wear jewelled bracelets and necklaces. A still more curious fact is that although the dancers invariably wore the skirt of tradi-tion, the supers were dressed in the correct costumes of the period of the ballet.

About 1904, a new apostle of the dance appeared in the person of Isadora Duncan. She condemned the traditional costume of the ballet, remarking that one does not play the piano with gloved hands, and hence the first essential for the liberation of the dance was to free the dancer from her short skirt, tight bodice, pink *maillot* and satin shoes. At this same time the young Russian *maître de ballet*, Mikhail Fokine, was consumed with a like desire to reform ballet costume and rescue it from its confusion of periods and styles, but he did not wish to destroy anything. He wanted Greek costumes, bare feet and flowing tresses for Greek ballets, the ballet skirt and *maillot* for the romantic ballets, Russian costumes for Russian ballets, and in time, aided by artists like Bakst, Benois, and Golovin, he succeeded in realising many of his ideals. The company of dancers directed by Serge Diaghileff has achieved a whole cycle of experiments in ballet costume, beginning with the gorgeous colour schemes of Bakst. His costume designs were vastly different from the conceptions of the nineteenth century. How often have we not seen those lifeless figures, each with faces and bodies almost exactly alike, whose clothes hang on them like a towel on a clothes-horse; and whose colour, crude and dingy at best, is almost effaced under a mass of florid detail ? How different from the figures of Bakst, which are almost a-quiver with life.

And what colours ! What European artist before Bakst ever employed colours so pure, so sparkling, and so animated; as a composer selects his key so he arranged his palette. And in the hands of an artist like Bakst, colour can be as potent as a drug. Pink cloys, one shade of green soothes, another jars, one tone of red maddens, black and violet depress, white purifies and chills—so Bakst played on the senses of the spectator and attuned his mood in harmony with the atmosphere required by the ballet.

The effect of the costumes at rest, in slow or rapid movement, was most carefully calculated. No physician ever drew up a prescription with greater regard for the combined effect of its constitutents than Bakst ordered his colours. And by cunning harmonies and contrasts of form and colour, he played on the spectator's emotions as a good actor can convey infinite degrees of joy or sorrow, passion or fear, by gesture and the varied tones of his voice. Bakst could be romantic as in " Les Femmes de Bonne Humeur "; sensuous, almost erotic, as in " Scheherazade "; mystical, as in " Le Dieu Bleu "; barbaric, as in " Thamar "; lyrical, as in " Narcisse." And though his costumes were never dull models of archæological exactitude, the most perfunctory examination of his designs reveals that the manners and customs of a people or an epoch had been studied thoroughly.

The conceptions of Bakst were followed by a series of contributions by Benois and Golovine, and by moderns such as Gontcharova, Sert, Picasso, Derain, Delaunay, Larionoff, Matisse, Laurencin, Braque, and Pruna.

THE PROBLEM OF THE DESIGNER

By James Laver

The ballet is the most composite of the arts. It is more composite even than opera, for singing is, after all, a form of music, whereas dancing, although music is its life-blood, is a form of nothing but itself. In opera, also, it is the ear that is ministered to—the eye grows dreamy; and so the *décor* of an opera does not hurt us badly even when it is as execrable as it almost invariably is. But in the ballet it is the ear which is relegated to second place. Dancing must be seen, and to see a dancer is to see his costume, and to be pleasantly or painfully aware—for one cannot be unaware —of his background. A harmonious ballet therefore, demands a triple miracle of agreement. It is a kind of *ménage à trois* of the arts of music, scene-painting, and choreography, and such *ménages* are notoriously difficult to conduct on, or off, the stage.

The main obstacle to harmony is that the arts are never at the same period of development; they will not keep pace, one or other always lags. The ripe romanticism of one corresponds, in point of time, with the frozen classicism of another; dancing is at its most formal just when painting has begun to concentrate upon the cruder emotions, and when music is preparing for Wagner. The problem of reconcilement is a difficult one, and it is to the credit of the Russians that they set themselves resolutely, with whatever varying degrees of success, to finding a solution, to constructing a satisfactory synthesis. There were, of course, ballets before Diaghileff, even modern ones attempting a certain sumptuousness of decoration. There were, for example, the entertainments provided at the Empire Theatre, London, at the beginning of the present century; but although some of Wilhelm's costumes for these were agreeably designed, the triteness of the themes—"Our Crown," or " Round the World "—and the lack of any powerful directing mind, tended to reduce them to mere dress parades.

There were the various schools of the " classical " ballet of which, perhaps, that at Milan touched the supremest heights of virtuosity, a virtuosity which was, as it were, a crystallisation of technique; something bright, and smooth, and shining—and quite dead. Against the stereotyped classical tradition there were solitary rebels, such as Isadora Duncan, chief of those who have been somewhat unkindly called " soul-dancers."

The Russian ballet as understood by Fokine was essentially a compromise, a blend of emotional and absolute dancing. It sought to give dancing a soul while preserving all the body's technical accomplishment. It sought to be danced emotion. Fokine himself, as most capable observers agree, lapsed in the intervals of dancing, into pantomime, into *acting*. It was Nijinsky, the supreme genius of the ballet, who danced everything, even his mimicry. But to all the principals of the Diaghileff Company expression was the essence of their art.

123

The transition, in short, from Petipa to Fokine, is the hatching from the egg of pure form of the active chicken of expressiveness. Something of the same thing happened in music between Bach and Beethoven, but the musical analogy is less important than the parallel with the art of painting. For the modern movement in painting is in precisely the opposite direction; it is a movement away from any kind of emotionalism, back to merely formal significance. It is a misfortune, therefore, that the plunge which dancing took, in our own day, into realism—for the stylising of emotion is as near realism as dancing can get, without ceasing to be dancing altogether—should have coincided with the reaction of painting towards abstract form. It was Diaghileff's determination only to employ the best, of all the arts he required, which made this difficulty apparent.

In the public mind the decorative artist most intimately linked with the Russian ballet is undoubtedly León Bakst. It was he who first introduced the eyes of Western Europe to a more than Oriental splendour of colouring in theatrical scenery and costume. It was he who cleared the contemporary stage of the dowdiness and dullness which audiences had endured too long. Yet the vigour and splendour of his scenes have no longer power to blind us to the fact that Bakst was a successful decorator of the ballet precisely because he was so old-fashioned. Here was no painful striving for formal significance, no reaching out towards the abstract, no preoccupation with volumes, and planes, and recessions. His originality consisted simply in his application of an Eastern luxury of colour to a very Western realism of design, and in his insistence on the unity of the stage-picture. It was his limitations which ensured his success. His work is admirable decoration, but it had nothing to do with the art of painting, as understood by our modern puritans of the easel.

Perhaps this was in the nature of things, and the Russians might have been saved some disappointment with the work of other artists if they had recognised earlier that it was so. The ballet is an artistic synthesis; and if all the arts, as Pater said, aspire to the condition of music, it is certain—although he did not say it—that they fall to complying with the conditions of literature. They can, so to say, meet on the musical plane, or on the literary plane. The first would be a miracle, inconceivable even until it had happened; the second is the common lot of those arts which compose the ballet. Literature, almost by definition, is bound to have the last *word*, even in a voiceless pantomime. What is *illustrated* is always a story, or a situation, that is, a story which is pausing to take breath. Literature is the thread on which the beads are strung.

The designer of dresses is, after all, chiefly concerned to transmit his directions to a dress-maker. Cubism, and similar theories of painting, are apt to obscure his intentions; and so we find that Gontcharova's cubist designs for Ravel's " Rhapsodie Espagnole " become, on the stage, costumes which a " naturalist " painter might well have conceived, save, perhaps, for some exaggerated emphasis on the folds and shadows of drapery. Picasso's backcloth for the " Tricorne " is a lovely thing, but how much does it owe to any of the successive theories which he has invented and abandoned. The painter must use a recognised idiom on pain of submitting to translation before his work is offered to the public. He cannot too often remember that he is but a collaborator, and that theatrical decoration is a branch of *applied* art. He should be grateful that his part in the construction is, to-day, such an important one; in the days of pure virtuoso dancing he was of no account at all. The once familiar ballet skirt was a crystallisation of costume, which made the dress-designer's office superfluous.

There was much to be said for the *tutu*, not indeed from the decorative artist's viewpoint, but from the dancer's. It left the limbs free, at least, and did not drag the body down with the weight of long skirts and wide panniers. But it cut the figure in two, transformed the wearer into a spinning top, and sacrificed at a stroke all possible appropriateness of costume. A ballet which strove to depict emotion was compelled to abandon the ballet skirt, and to substitute for it the thousand varied costumes which gave Bakst and Benois, Roerich, and Soudeikine their opportunity. The modern designer is not confined to any traditional style; he has all the world before him, subject only to the necessity of leaving the limbs as free as possible. Perhaps we shall not be far wrong if we say that the costume ideal for ballet is nudity tempered by the suggestion of a period.

Our new sensitiveness to " period " is one of the most powerful weapons in the armoury of the decorative artist. How new such a feeling is, Garrick's powdered Macbeth bears witness; but the nineteenth century developed a strong historical sense in all educated people, and we have now grown so sophisticated that we can throw off mere historical accuracy, and enjoy the exquisite pleasure of regarding one period through the eyes of another. Archæology becomes dull through excessive familiarity, and we begin to appreciate a conscious falsification of period, as when Sert and Bakst conspire to dress Potiphar's wife as a sixteenth-century Venetian, and to set her against a scene copied from a Veronese banquet. The device must be used with caution, or the ballet degenerates into the tasteless chaos of a fancy dress ball. To one spectator, at least, the Chinaman in " Pompeii à la Massine " seemed wholly a mistake. There must be a predominant flavour, if the word may be permitted, and such anachronisms as do occur must be admitted only as seasoning. In this connection it is interesting to note that even the *tutu* has now become costume again, because it evokes a definite period, has become redolent of a past epoch, as in " Les Sylphides."

In general, the decorator will find that " period "—the word being used in its widest sense—is dictated to him by the arranger of the ballet, or by the author upon whose scenario the ballet has been founded. Even with a well-known subject, however, great liberty is often permitted. Soudeikine's decorations of " Salomé " had no perceptible connection with the Judæa of Herod. His costume for the princess herself (danced by the

Karsavina) was as pure a work of fantasy as Beardsley's illustrations to Wilde; and few would deny that it is better for the artist to work out his own conception rather than to attempt any precise and lifeless archæological reconstruction. Yet he complicates his own problem by departing too widely from the obvious *décor* of a subject, because he is then compelled to take entirely upon his own shoulders the difficult task of evoking in an audience the mood which the theme demands.

It is only within recent years that mood in theatrical decoration has received from artists the attention it deserves. The spirit of a play—even of a realistic play—does seem to be reflected in certain colours rather than in others, and the decorator should choose such appropriate colours for the dominant notes of his scene-painting. As regards costume, this truth has long been recognised—Hamlet is traditionally black-suited—but its systematic application to the whole stage-picture is of more recent date. It has been most completely worked out in theory by Mr. Gordon Craig, although Seymour Lucas, writing as long ago as the early 'nineties, advised artists to paint the scene for " Ravenswood " in sombre greys, and that for " Henry VIII " in red and gold.

Ernst Stern, who has done so much work for Reinhardt, tries to suggest mood not only by colour, but by line, making successful play with the perpendiculars of Gothic, or the writhing curves of the Baroque. By this means he avoids too great insistence on any one colour, however appropriate; for, as Noverre recognised long ago, there must be some contrast between the painted scene and the actor's costume, or else the eye is fatigued, and, if a dancer remains motionless for an instant, he is lost to sight altogether. A nice balance, indeed, between figure and background reveals, more than anything else, the hand of the master.

The principals in a ballet will, if they are worthy of their place, stand out from the crowd of figurants by the force of their own talents. The designer, however, can do something to increase their pre-eminence, and to concentrate the attention of the audience upon them, by skilful gradations in the colour of the costumes. It is sometimes effective to dress everyone in a different shade of the same colour, reserving the brightest hues for the most important characters; or the chorus can be attired very gorgeously, and the principals very simply, or all in white. The important thing is that no costume should be considered or designed by itself, but always with reference to its place in the complete stage-picture.

Noverre's chief problem in the gradation of colour need not trouble the modern designer at all. He was principally concerned with giving the illusion of perspective, and so he wished the costumes of those most distant from the audience to be darker, to have more blue in them, than those nearer to the footlights, just as if they were figures in a real landscape. Once, at least, he even went so far as to employ children instead of adults at the back of the stage, in order not to falsify the exaggerated perspective of the painted scenery. Modern audiences have grown tired of the elaborate scenic backcloth and are content, for the most part, with a shallow stage, without painted vistas. So much more can be suggested by modern lighting than was possible in the days of oil or gas, that a laboriously painted naturalistic backdrop no longer seems the ultimate triumph of scenic art.

Lighting, indeed, is sure to be used more and more, in conjunction with scene-painting, in all kinds of theatrical decoration. The illuminated waving skirts of Loïe Fuller were a portent; and the new devices—used so far only as music-hall tricks—by which the colours, and even the forms, of costumes may be made to change, are symptomatic of the novel importance in the theatre of the man at the electric switch-board. There are even those who are so tired of naturalistic effects that they clamour for " the cold, clear vitality of electricity itself, the electric bulb in all its powerful nudity "; and regard Picabia's " Relâche " as the end to which all the artists of the theatre have laboured throughout the ages. But such a snobbery of asceticism is unlikely to last.

The cinema, that other art of gesture, will probably influence the actual technique of the ballet, not only by suggesting postures and movements—as in Cocteau's " Train Bleu," when the entire *corps de ballet* imitated the slow-motion film—but by providing, perhaps, the most satisfactory method yet invented of recording dance-steps. That it will, however, affect the problem of the designer is more doubtful, although it may provide him occasionally with a moving background, similar in effect to the dioramas of the early nineteenth century. In any case mechanical inventions render more necessary than ever the directing hand of the artist. Fortunate indeed is the modern stage designer, if he can rise to his opportunities, for his palette is composed, not only of every pigment in the colour-box, but of every hue in the rainbow.

COSTUME IN BALLET

By Edith Carlyon

The evolution of ballet from the dullness and convention of its earliest theatrical forms into a vital and living art is largely due to the changes in costume which have been effected at different stages in its development.

The ballet of the theatre, in its early days, bore a strong resemblance to the ballets of the French Court, from which it originated. There was very little story or plot, but magnificent scenes and pageants were interspersed between the acts of the operas, having no relation to the opera itself, and very often the various scenes of the ballet were quite independent of each other, and simply presented a spectacle of magnificent scenery, gorgeous dresses, and wonderful mechanical effects.

In the seventeenth century, when Louis XIV founded L'Académie Royale de Danse, so little was the art of ballet understood, and so strong were the ties of convention, that the dancers, whoever they represented, and in whatever scenes they appeared, always wore the elegant and exaggerated costumes of their own period. They were so elaborately dressed that they must have found it rather difficult to move at all, and consequently their technique was very limited. And as their faces were always covered with masks, they could not use facial expression to help their actions. The audience must have found it rather wearying to watch a set of " mask " expressions, grinning or sober, as the case might be, dancing their way through the entire ballet without the slightest change, until the mask itself was changed.

Dresses and masks belonged to convention, which was strictly observed. The women wore dresses made with tightly fitting bodices, sometimes pointed at the front and back, thus giving an exceedingly slender appearance to the waist; from the waist downwards, however, they became enormous in size, and hoops and panniers of every description were worn, completely disguising the real contours of the figure. And their sleeves were padded into all kinds of peculiar shapes and sizes. The men were dressed as elaborately as the women; coats were made to fit tightly at the waist, and were set out from the hips by padding, breeches reached to the knee, and silk stockings were worn with decorated garters.

There was a great vogue for embroidery, which extended to almost every article of clothing, including shoes. Dresses and coats were embroidered with flowers, leaves, stars, and many other devices, and shoes were also adorned with rosettes or buckles, and had very high heels. Tinsel and spangles were used profusely in the costumes, to make the effect as gorgeous as possible.

The coiffures were varied, and often very absurd. A woman of the eighteenth century might wear a head-dress reaching to the height of eighteen inches! The styles of hairdressing were exceedingly complicated, and the huge erections were crowned with flowers, ribbons, pearls and ostrich plumes. Powdered and curled wigs were worn by both men and women,

T   129

but the women usually required the aid of pads and wired frames to keep their head-dresses in place. Hats, and the helmets of the men, were also adorned with plumes and tufts of feathers.

The extravagance and artificiality of the costumes were in keeping with the kind of ballet presented at the French Opera, in which mythological and allegorical characters of every description appeared. Gods and demons, fauns and naiads, winds, fires and dreams, were all dressed very similarly, the colours and ornaments of their costumes being the main points of difference. And they all performed dances quite unsuited to their characters, and rather monotonous in their sequence. But at that time it did not occur to anyone to inquire why they dressed like that, or why they danced in that particular way. It was considered the correct thing to do, and so they did it !

About the same period, the latter half of the seventeenth and beginning of the eighteenth centuries, some superb designs were produced in Vienna, where the whole art of production in the theatre was at its height, and nothing seemed impossible. This was in the age of Leopold I, the classical age of theatrical production which " Placed the whole of nature on the stage, just as it presented the whole of history and mythology." Colour, warmth, rich and variegated materials, and sumptuous ornaments marked the costumes, and although they invariably followed contemporary fashion, as in the French theatre, yet far more imagination and fantasy were shown in the designs, and the nature of the costume was shown by various accessories which were skilfully introduced into the general scheme. For instance, a costume designed for Pallas Athene showed the outline of the contemporary dress, and tight-fitting bodice and wide skirt, etc., but the head-dress bore the suggestion of a helmet, and other details of the costume suggested various attributes of the goddess.

These dresses, were also covered with beautiful embroideries, but the motifs of these had nothing to do with the origin of the costume; a dress embroidered with devices of shells and seaweed did not indicate that its wearer was a nymph, or anything connected with the sea. Some of the costumes were purely fantastic, and seemed to belong to a gay magic world of their own, far apart from everyday life. And there were quaint examples of flower costumes and feather costumes. These flower and feather motifs have been used frequently in theatrical costume, and many variations of them have been seen, especially in ballet.

To return to France, where a pall of monotony hung over the costumes and dances, and inspiration was sadly needed to give life and meaning to the ballet. Early in the eighteenth century, Jean Georges Noverre was born in Paris. Noverre has been called " The Shakespeare of the Dance," and he banished the outworn traditions of the ballet, and in their place created a thing of surpassing beauty. He saw the talent that was being wasted because it had no outlet, and he implored the dancers to leave off their masks, wigs and helmets, their panniers and padded coats, and to dance with their bodies free and their faces uncovered. He pointed out the absurdity of a shepherd dancing in a plumed helmet, of a warrior appearing after a combat as though he had just come forth from a careful and an immaculate toilet; and the general impediment to the dancer's ability caused by so many unnecessary trappings.

These new ideas did not meet with approval for a long time. Sallé, a great *danseuse* of the eighteenth century, had already tried to effect a costume reform at the Opera in Paris, but she was not allowed to carry out her ideas. She rebelled against convention, but convention was too strong for her, so she went to London, and there she danced in classic draperies. Jullien, in his History of Theatrical Costume, describes her appearance in London in the ballet of "Pygmalion," without the customary panniers and voluminous petticoats, without any ornament on her head, but simply clad in drapery of the Greek style, and she met with an enthusiastic reception. London was not so bound by convention as Paris, and was more receptive of new ideas. And although Noverre was a Frenchman, born in Paris, it was not until he had won fame in foreign lands, and exerted his influence on the ballet in foreign capitals, that he was allowed to use this influence in his own country.

But gradually genius triumphed, and changes began to take place, even in Paris. The mask was first discarded in 1772. On this occasion Gaetan Vestris was to represent a fair-haired Apollo in an enormous black wig, a mask, and wearing a large gilded sun on his breast. For some reason he was unable to play his part, and Maximilien Gardel offered to take his place on condition that he should appear in his own fair hair, without the mask and the gilded sun. He did so, and created such a sensation that the leading actors began to play without masks from that time, though the chorus still wore them for some years.

Through the influence of Noverre, ballet gradually became transformed into a thing of artistic beauty. The costumes became more in keeping with the characters represented, and at the same time adapted to the requirements of the dance. The tight-fitting bodice remained, but the panniers and padding disappeared, giving place, in some instances, to long skirts of light gauzy material, which later developed into the ballet-dress of the Victorian era. The ridiculous head-dresses also vanished, and the hair was dressed in a simple manner, high off the forehead.

This reformation in costume was a great factor in the development of the technique of the dance. Camargo, a contemporary of Sallé, and Noverre, found that her long skirts interfered with the execution of her steps, and so she shortened them until they reached above her ankles. This led to the discovery of all kinds of new steps and movements; Camargo was famous for her brilliant technique, a great deal of which had been made possible by the simple process of shortening her skirts!

The progress of ballet was checked temporarily by the Revolution, but early in the nineteenth century Milan became the centre of interest, and took the lead under the guidance of another great *Maître de Ballet*, Carlo Blasis. Many big continental schools were influenced by the method of training which Blasis instituted at La Scala, Milan, and, with the help and encouragement which he gave to all of his profession with whom he came in contact, fresh artistic triumphs were achieved.

Of the five great *danseuses* of this golden age of ballet, three were Italian, one was Austrian, and one Danish; and the greatest of these was an Italian, Marie Taglioni. Her art was spiritual and poetical in nature, and she is generally represented in pictures and engravings in a long white ballet-dress of muslin, her hair often adorned with a wreath of roses. This style of dress was worn by *ballerinas* for a long time, but a *danseuse* who was engaged to appear in Petrograd flatly refused to dance in a long skirt, and defied the rules of the theatre by cutting her dress short. Gradually the long skirts grew shorter and shorter, to lengthen again into the ballet-dress that is worn at the present period.

After the passing of Taglioni, a period of dullness followed, during which nothing of outstanding merit was produced, and it was not until the end of the nineteenth century that a revival took place, when the days of the English ballet began. Hitherto, the Haymarket, Covent Garden, and Her Majesty's theatres had been associated with it, but the Empire and the Alhambra were to be the homes of the English ballet. In the 'eighties of last century ballet became a regular feature of the programme at these two theatres, and continued to be so for over twenty years.

The success of these productions was very largely due to the beauty and variety of the costumes which were designed by Mr. C. Wilhelm. Mr. Wilhelm was a considerable artist of the theatre. Perhaps the public sometimes forget how much they owe to the artists behind the scenes, who do their work before the show commences, and do not personally receive the plaudits of the public.

Mr. Francis M. Kelly, who assisted Mr. Wilhelm for some years at the Empire theatre, gives very interesting accounts of how the work was carried on there. An intimate knowledge of a constant personnel was naturally a great advantage, and Mr. Wilhelm always visualised exactly how his costumes would look on the people for whom they were intended, before he commenced to execute his designs; and woe betide the unfortunate person who failed to wear her costume as it should be worn, thus ruining the effect of a beautiful design. He thoroughly understood the technique of dressmaking, and this ensured that the execution of his designs should be carried out correctly in every detail, as he was able to give the most precise instructions to the costumier about colour and material. He was especially interested in "period" subjects, and designed some exquisite costumes after the style of Watteau and Lancret, for "Fête Galante" and "Pastorale," in which the spirit of that beautiful French period lived again in the costumes, music and dances.

"Les Papillons" was another very charming ballet, and in this the butterfly and insect costumes made a splendid riot of colour, the butterfly wings with their delicate markings being especially beautiful.

" Old China " dealt with the romance of a little Dresden china shepherd-ess, and the dancers were dressed to represent old china figures; and again an exquisite illusion was created. The second scene was called " Willow Pattern Land " ! Some magnificent spectacular ballets were presented, the most notable of which were " Versailles " (1892), " Faust " (1895), and " Monte Cristo " (1896), and for each of these Mr. Wilhelm was respon-sible for the scenario as well as for the costumes.

Some beautiful ballets were produced at the Alhambra, with costumes designed by Comelli, and others; but the excellence of the *tout ensemble* at the Empire theatre, made the Empire ballets memorable in the history of ballet in England.

Two more ballets, which must not be omitted when speaking of the English ballet, were presented at the London Coliseum, namely, " La Danse," and " Camargo." In the former, the *danseuses* and dances of the past, from the beginning of the eighteenth century to the middle of the nineteenth, were re-created, the famous *danseuses* of each period being impersonated by Madame Genee in her incomparable way, against the beautiful settings provided by Mr. Wilhelm.

A few years before the war, a new phase of the art of ballet was seen in England. But it is not yet time to write of the Russians in retrospect, and the wonderful designs of Leon Bakst are well known to-day to all who have eyes for beauty. This is only a very brief survey of costume in connexion with ballet in past years; it is a subject which cannot be dealt with very fully in a short space, but has an endless fascination for those who have the time and inclination to study it.

PLATE LXXXI.

GLYN PHILPOT, R.A.

"Warrior"

For Negro Ballet.

PLATE LXXXI

GLYN PHILPOT, R.A.
" Warrior."
For Negro Ballet.

PLATE LXXXII

CECIL FFRENCH SALKELD
" Oriental Woman."

PLATE LXXXIII

CECIL FFRENCH SALKELD
" Oriental Potentate.'

PLATE LXXXIV

CECIL FFRENCH SALKELD
"Grotesque."

PLATE LXXXIV

CECIL FFRENCH SALKELD
" Grotesque."

PLATE LXXXV

PAUL NASH
Design for Costume for Madame Karsavina.
For Sir James Barrie's " The Truth about the Russian Dancers."

Design for Costume for
Madame Karsavina.

PLATE LXXXVI

PAUL NASH
Costume for the Corps-de-Ballet.
For Sir James Barrie's " The Truth about the Russian Dancers."

Costume
for
The Corps de Ballet
"The Truth about
the Russian
Dancers."

1920

PLATE LXXXVII

GLADYS SPENCER CURLING
" Enigma."

PLATE LXXXVIII

BRIDGET EVANS
"Warrior."
For "Fairy Tale Ballet."

REGINALD LEEFE
"Indian Warrior."

PLATE LXXXIX

PAUL ROTHA
" The Vizard Mask."

REGINALD LEEFE
" The Shah."

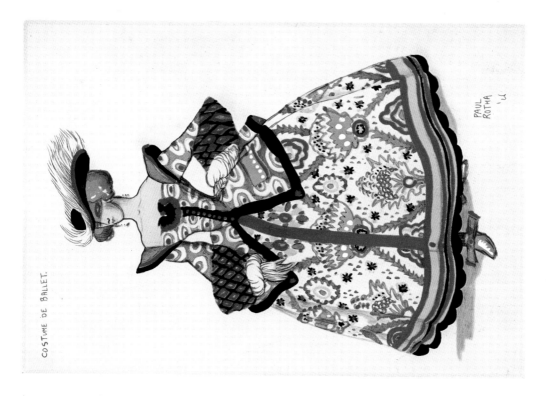

COSTUME DE BALLET.

PAUL
ROTHA
'U

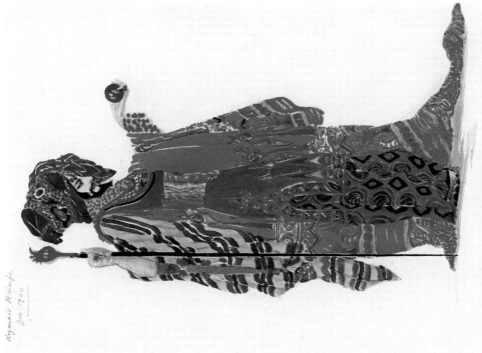

Reginald Hodge
Dec 1924

PLATE XC

LAURENCE BRADSHAW
" Modern Harlequinade."

Laurence Bradshaw
1926

PLATE XCI

PHYLLIS DOLTON
" Shepherdesses."
For " The Jealous Shepherd."

ELSPETH ANNE LITTLE
" Dancer's Dress " (Painted).

Phyllis E. Walton 1926

Elspeth Anne Little

PLATE XCII

PHYLLIS DOLTON
" Anne and Jeanne."
For " Barbe Bleau."

PLATE XCIII

PHYLLIS DOLTON
" Chloris."
For " The Jealous Shepherd."

Phyllis E. Dolton
1926

PLATE XCIV

PHYLLIS DOLTON
" Charmides."
For " The Jealous Shepherd."

PLATE XCV

ELSPETH ANNE LITTLE
" Design for Eighteenth Century Dress."

Elspeth Anne Little

PLATE XCVI

ELSPETH ANNE LITTLE
" Smoking Suit "
(Painted and Printed).

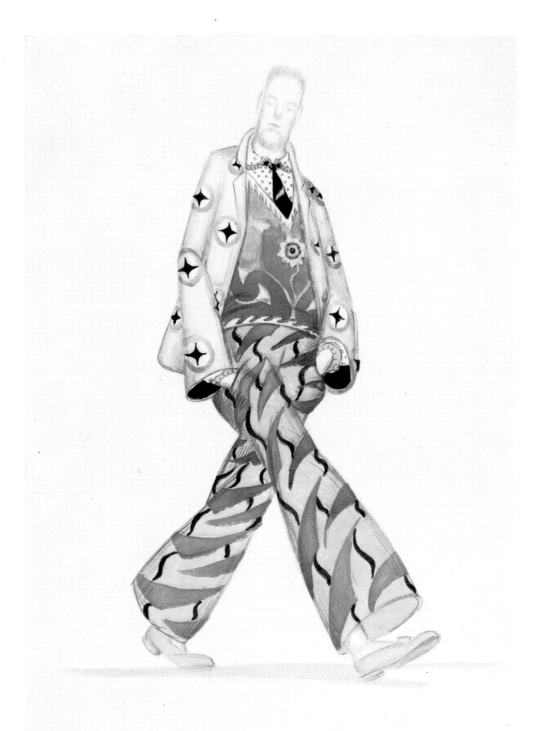

Elspeth Anne Little

PLATE XCVII

ELSPETH ANNE LITTLE
"Man's Woodpecker Costume."

Elspeth Anne Little

PLATE XCVIII

D. W. DRING
" The Archer."

WILLIAM DRING 1926.

PLATE XCIX

D. W. DRING
" Chinoiserie."

WILLIAM ORPEN 1926.

PLATE C

D. W. DRING
" A Fallen Angel."

PLATE CI

D. W. DRING
" Cain."

WILLIAM DRING 1926.

PLATE CII

LAURA KNIGHT, A.R.A.

Crowd and Scotch Dancer.

For " The Goose Fair."

A farmer and son lived in a very lonely country place. The farmer was afraid of his son marrying and leaving him, so he never took him where there were any women. The result was that the boy had never seen a woman until it became necessary for them both to go to a fair, held at the nearest town, to dispose of their farm produce. The farmer promised to give his son a fairing. On arriving, the first person they met was a woman. " What is that? " said the son. " A goose," said the farmer. When they had disposed of their goods, the farmer asked his son what he would like for a fairing. " A goose ! " said the son.

Crowd and Scotch Dancer

L·K

PLATE CIII

LAURA KNIGHT, A.RA.
" Fat Lady, Strong Man, and Human Serpent."
For " The Goose Fair."

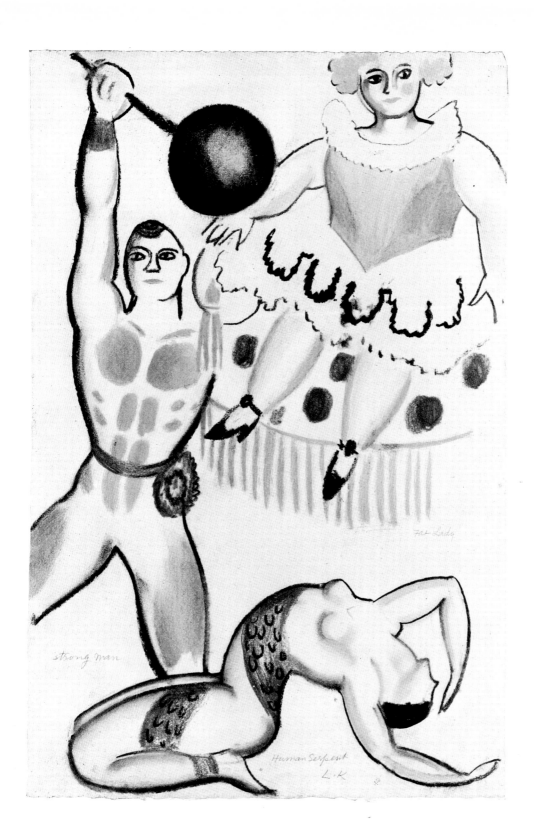

strong man

Fat Lady

Human Serpent
L.K.

PLATE CIV

LAURA KNIGHT, A.R.A.
" Cyclist, Policeman, and Orangewoman."
For " The Goose Fair."

Cyclist, Policeman
and orange woman

IX
THE ARTIST IN THE DRESSING ROOM

THE ARTIST IN THE DRESSING ROOM

By Horace Shipp

Unfortunately in the English theatre it is not yet a matter for amazed laughter to discover on one's programme, between the description of scenes and the demands of the Lord Chamberlain, a veritable directory of modistes, furriers, shoemakers, furniture dealers, musical instrument firms and other no doubt honest tradesfolk whose products have contributed to the *mise en scène*. This reciprocation of borrowing and publicity offends neither our sense of dignity nor of art. In truth, in a theatre so frankly commercial as our own, governed almost entirely by an æsthetic or naturalistic representation, there can be little offence in such a phenomenon and no surprise, unless surprise comes on those occasions when we find that on this matter of decoration and costume an artist has been requisitioned. Happily these occasions grow more frequent. The campaign for an all-embracing art of the theatre, an art in which the dramatist's intention finds interpretation not alone by the actor's contribution, but visually by the scene designer, the costumier and the lighting mechanician—that campaign has had increasing effect upon the stages of Europe and England. If we review the progress from the barren period of the nineteenth century we realise how truly enormous the advance has been; we can claim with satisfaction that alongside of the ordinary theatre, dealing purely in amusement, exists a minority theatre earnest in its study of the problems of its complex art, making some effort to encourage its audiences to accept the best drama, and calling in the aid of the artist-decorator in his capacity of scene designer, and of costume designer, to ensure a worthy result. Moreover, even the majority theatre, which avows no allegiance to the theories of Craig, Appia,

Stanislavski, Reinhardt, Georg Fuchs, Antoine or Copeau, has not been uninfluenced. The artist has taken his place in the theatre.

In considering his appearance there in the guise of costumier, one has first to take cognisance of the broad division of artistic purpose which has operated throughout the whole history of recent theatre reform. Most sharply defined probably in Russia in the respective theories of Stanislavski and of Meyerhold, this division lies between a search for greater realistic truth and greater stylisation; and it is an interesting paradox that whichever line individual reformers took, the theatre was the richer. On the one hand there came the great wave of the naturalistic drama, with names like Ibsen, Hauptmann and Tchekhov, giving an entirely new content to European drama, and demanding for their presentation truth of realistic setting and costume; on the other we find a theatre of revolt against the prose of this drama, turning to any which offered beauty, fantasy, colour and a definite art form. When we compare their work to the false and forced theatricalism which preceded it, we realise how great a service the early realists performed to the art they so conscientiously served; and even though these pioneers themselves tended to turn from mere naturalism to symbolism and poetic drama, even though we now realise how much deeper Ibsen's work went, or what significance there is behind Tchekhov's seeming naturalism, one must pay passing tribute to the school. It accepted the important theory that the visual drama must be perfect in detail, expressive and interpretative of the author's intention; and scene and costume were studied to this end.

An interesting by-product of this philosophy of theatrical truth, so far as costume was concerned, was the institution by Herbert Beerbohm Tree in 1882 of the Costume Society.

Concerned in particular with Shakespearean production, he demanded exact archæological truth to the Shakespeare dresses, and the society did useful work in research into the whole subject, although in the modern reaction against realism in the art theatre these Tree productions, and his search for convincing realistic details, are regarded as anathema and maranatha. In justice to him, however, it is necessary to compare his productions and his costumes with those of the end of last century rather than with the Savoy productions of Granville Barker in 1912.

It was, however, rather upon the turn of the tide of this naturalism and historic exactness that the artist really was piloted into the theatre. The Ibsen controversy had raged and ended, the Stage Society with all that it implied was *fait accompli*, the sociological drama of Shaw, the middle-class realism of Galsworthy and Barker had been established at the famous Court seasons; Miss Horniman's Repertory Theatre at Manchester had so allied itself with the tragic realism of lower middle-class and working-class existence that this type of play was connoted by the terms " Repertory " and " Manchester "; realism was in full flood. It would be difficult now to say from whence came the currents which set in towards a theatre of beauty.

Not from one source, probably, unless that source were the urgent need of men's hearts for something more than bread alone whereby to live. Craig's productions during the first three years of the century, and his continuous propaganda, the performances of " Sumuran," of " The Miracle," and of " Oedipus Rex," under Max Reinhardt, the Barker productions of Shakespeare, decorated and dressed by Albert Rutherston and Norman Wilkinson, the establishment of the Birmingham Repertory Theatre, the coming of the Russian Ballet evidenced and encouraged the reaction. Other theatres and other work, both professional and amateur, reiterated and echoed the tendency; the lighter productions in the commercial theatres accepted the need of the artist as designer of costume and scene, and in all branches easel painters of repute began to serve the theatre.

To-day it would be almost impossible to make an exhaustive survey of the activities of the artist-costumier. The work of certain men and of certain theatres will immediately establish claims. Nigel Playfair's productions at Hammersmith and elsewhere, and those of the ballet are so conspicuous as to warrant special sections of this volume, and in these will be found notice of the work of such outstanding artists as Claud Lovat Fraser, William Nicholson, George Sheringham, Norman Wilkinson and others, as well as those of the great artists who have worked under Diaghileff. Beside these one must consider the exquisite work of the Birmingham Repertory, certain productions of the Reandean management where beauty or originality of costume have been demanded, and much work under the Cassons. Even the opera has occasionally broken from its devastating traditions, whilst the Coliseum has given us a Barrie fantasy with costumes by so advanced a person as Paul Nash, and the revues are now as likely to present an exquisite Hogarth ballet dressed by Nicholson as to tittilate the groundlings with Spinelli in an ostrich feather cloak which reveals her back bare to the waist. Nor does the cult of the costume stop with the West End. At the Old Vic., where John Garside and his confreres have created a marvellous silk purse from a sow's ear by remodelling the wardrobe; at Norwich, the Maddermarket theatre; at Oxford, the Playhouse, under J. B. Fagan; at Cambridge, the Festival Theatre; at Manchester, the work of the Unnamed Society; at Liverpool, that of the Repertory Theatre, under William Armstrong; everywhere the need is felt and catered for. The list drifts lightly over the professional stage to that of the amateurs and the community groups. It is, indeed, frequently these who are most artistically alive; and the days when all that amateurs asked was the opportunity of acting the rôles of people who wore dress clothes every evening, have almost disappeared. In their place we have groups of amateurs so conscious of the artistic needs of their self-imposed task that their work constitutes a veritable campaign for a theatre of beauty. One need only mention such names as the Stockport Garrick Society, Citizen House Theatre at Bath, The Studio Theatre of London and Swanage under Mrs. Spencer Watson, The Greenleaf Theatre of the Maxwell Armfields, or the Glastonbury

Festival to establish this claim; and the network of such theatres across the country is one of the important elements in theatre organisation of to-day.

In this matter of costuming, the Birmingham theatre takes indisputable first rank. Evolving from an amateur society, The Pilgrim Players under the direction of Barry V. Jackson, the Birmingham Repertory Theatre has from the start been an art theatre in the connotation of a theatre which is primarily concerned with the drama of poetry and beauty rather than that of realism. The opportunity for the costumier has, therefore, always been great. Indeed it would be fair to say that the policy of this theatre—that of doing the imaginative type of play with frequent change of programme in the repertory manner—has given greater scope for the artist than is to be found in any theatre in England. This is evidenced by the fact that Paul Shelving, the artist of the theatre, has the designs of just over a hundred productions to his credit, all but seven of which have been Birmingham Repertory plays. In a few years the name of Paul Shelving has taken its place firmly with those of the English stage decorators and costumiers, as the Birmingham Repertory Theatre has established itself both in Birmingham and in London at the Kingsway, Court and Regent Theatres.

His work is typical of that of the English theatre artists. The varying demands of the stage for which he works has given him extraordinary versatility, ranging between the selective realism of "Manchester School" drama and the Expressionism of Georg Kaiser's "Gas." What Mr. Wyndham Lewis would call his vortex, however, is in decoration. Thus he will tend to create a beautifully coloured, semi-naturalistic rendering of the scenes of the play; and his costumes, semi-naturalistic and highly coloured also, are designed as part of this scene. Naturally the piece dictates how far he may bring this decorative sense into play, but the draw of the vortex brings a touch of emerald green and vermilion into the drabbest Lancastrian kitchen under his hands, and the abstraction of Kaiser's play was toned down to something much more decorous than any German artist would have produced. Given Goldoni or Sheridan, Shakespeare, such a fifteenth century piece as " The Marvellous History of Saint Bernard," Shaw's " Cæsar and Cleopatra," the more coloured parts of the Methuselah Cycle, or the romance and barbarism of " The Immortal Hour," however; Shelving will design exquisitely coloured and shaped dresses harmonising his figures perfectly with the scenes and in a broad way with the play motive.

It may well be a matter for dispute whether the costume designer can ever do more than this. In the English theatre, certainly, the demand for more scarcely ever arises. The scene if it escapes naturalism goes no further than decoration. The *decor vivant* of Craig's dream, the abstraction of Expressionism or of such artistic experiments as Synthesism, Futurism, Cubism, have found no place on the English stage, so that our costume designers faced with their task of forming a liaison between the human factor and the scene have invariably been able to solve their problem in terms of decoration. Costumes such as those designed by Prampolini in

Italy, by Tairov for the Kamerny Theatre, or by the exponents of the advanced theatre in Central Europe and here and there in America, are unknown and untried. The success of any methods far removed from naturalism is by the nature of the case doubtful, for the human body remains intractable into any work of abstract art, and only when the acting, the movements and gestures are denaturalised to synthesise with a *decor* of absolute convention can the costumier create clothes based upon such an æsthetic.

In his decorative costumes, therefore, Paul Shelving is strictly in the English modern tradition. Fantasy and charm, beauty and purity of form there are in his work, with a delight in the details, but, nevertheless, a unity and breadth of artistic purpose. No artist can better create a period without slavishly imitating its archæological facts, and within the limits of the method of decoration, no artist can better interpret a character or the psychic motives of a drama.

This triumph of artistic performance achieved within a stricture of artistic purpose applies to practically all the best men working on the costumes of the English stage. Charles Ricketts' name is probably better known to the general public as a stage dress designer than that of any other artist save Lovat Fraser. His artistry is less conscious than that of Fraser, his truth to period more detailed, but his genius for making the clothes complete the design of his scene is outstanding. His recent success with " The Mikado," or earlier with Shaw's " Saint Joan" made the public aware as they seldom are of the presence of an artist-costumier. Shaw's play gave an excellent opportunity; its fine period, its many characters and their tremendous range could not but delight an artist in dresses. And this opportunity Ricketts grasped. His method was more exactly archæological than the younger school of decorators would have been likely to bring to the task; the rich stuffs and splendid patternings of the fifteenth century, and the infinite variety of form and tone which the court, the church, the army and the people actually placed to his hand demanding little more than cohesion and synthesis into his pictures. His method of scene designing, which gives his stage height at the expense of depth, is tremendously helped by the kaleidoscopic movement of a frieze of brightly coloured costume across the stage, and some of his best pictures are attained by this means. Charles Ricketts' work is seen all too seldom on the stage. One needs but to remember his early contribution when, under Herbert Trench's inspired management of the Haymarket, Ricketts dressed Maeterlinck's " Blue Bird," his "Judith," or his comparatively recent "Macbeth" to realise that the theatre has a splendid recruit in this fine artist.

"Saint Joan" and "Macbeth" were produced under the Casson management, which has given to the stage some of the finest work of our generation. A premier part for Sybil Thorndike may be the dictating element in the choice of their plays, but with this justifiable limitation their bias is towards the poetic and imaginative drama. When the exigencies of the commercial theatre precluded such drama from the regular bill, they have offered it at special performances and matinees, alone or in conjunction with the producing groups and societies. With such drama the artist of scene and costume has his place. Under the Cassons, with their artistic creed of the paramount importance of acting and play, this place may have tended to be slightly narrowed, but it has never been neglected. Their memorable matinees of Greek plays, the productions of Shelley's "Cenci," Toller's expressionistic "Masse Mensch," are but a few of these. Working with them as designer and maker of costumes they have Bruce Winston. I do not know whether Mr. Winston would claim to be the artist in the dressing room; rather, I imagine, he would regard himself as the ordinary habitant of that region turned costume artist to suit the needs of the case. But the result is excellent. Bruce Winston's costumes belong to the theatre; they have a touch of the theatricalism of a day before the artist-costumier was known, and because of this they merge into these particular productions and do not suffer so much when Lewis Casson succumbs to his tendency to do somewhat wild things with his lights. The "Masse Mensch" production was of special interest to the student of theatre art in that it exemplified the English way with an expressionistic play. In Berlin, as a Fehling production with Hans Strohbach's designs, it had been a piece of pure abstraction, arbitrarily lighted by intersecting beams, with scenes and costumes of entirely unreal colour. Here the abstraction approached much nearer to a decorative symbolism, and the costumes, of course, were designed in this spirit. They were more colourful, more emotional, less intellectual. Bruce Winston's costumes on this occasion were seen in settings designed by Aubrey Hammond, himself a costume artist whose work is often seen in the lighter type of production and shows an ingenious fancifulness.

Another management which during recent years served the theatre of decoration was the Reandean. During the few years wherein they functioned at their home at the St. Martin's Theatre, or in the varying houses which have come under his artistic control Basil Dean contributed much to contemporary theatre history. The costumes and the scenes for his productions are invariably designed by George W. Harris, an artist of amazing versatility, although his artistic individuality is not pronounced. Now and again, as for example when he had the big opportunity with Basil Dean's superproduction of "The Midsummer Night's Dream" at Drury Lane, he can become a creative artist. The brilliant costumes for the final scene for this, placed against the dazzling whiteness of the finely conceived palace, were a triumph. Also one remembers his dresses for Clemence Dane's "Queen Elizabeth," his clever imaginative costumes for the Robots in Karel Capek's "R.U.R." and his work elsewhere throughout the series of Reandean plays. In spite of a high level and a decided stageworthiness, however, it too often plays for safety and so loses individuality.

The thought of "The Midsummer Night's Dream" and Mr. Harris's mounting of it evokes the memory of the Old Vic. production of the same play which ran contemporaneously with it. One could not but feel that John Garside's pure artistry and narrow means pitted against the thousands of pounds which had been lavished at Drury Lane constituted in result an absolute triumph for the artist. The Old Vic. Shakespearean wardrobe had undergone amazing metamorphosis under his hands and those of Robert Atkins, the producer there, and only those who know how this theatre has to make pence do the work of pounds will fully appreciate the staging and costuming of the complete Shakespearean repertoire and such incidentals as " Peer Gynt," Goethe's " Faust," or Halcott Glover's " Wat Tyler."

This slight and necessarily incomplete record of the coming of the artist-costumier into the English theatre will serve, if it does no more than indicate his accepted presence there. Because, on the whole, he has come with no outre or bizarre æsthetic, but has trodden the path of a decorated naturalism, we have taken so easily to the innovation that we have scarcely noticed it. Occasionally, as when Granville Barker carried matters a distinct step forward with the aid of Albert Rutherston and Norman Wilkinson and startled us into realisation with the gold fairies of the " Midsummer Night's Dream," or when Paul Nash dressed Barrie's " The Truth about the Russian Ballet " at the original Coliseum production, or when the Birmingham people achieve a *succes de scandale* by dressing Hamlet in plus fours, we realise that somebody is taking this business of clothes in the theatre seriously. Occasionally at the lightest revue we find this unexpected link with that earnest art theatre of which we are cognisant at the Russian Ballet productions, or in the most self-conscious foreign playhouses; sometimes an amateur group in some remote place will be found working with an inspired artist designer; sometimes a Sunday play-producing Society will feel that the play demands the hand of the artist in its mounting. But, however and whenever his coming, those of us who love the theatre and dream of it as an art in itself will feel our hopes one step nearer fulfilment as we watch the artist as costumier come into his kingdom.

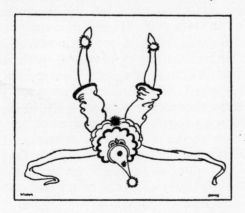

PLATE CV

DOROTHY MULLOCK
" Pia Giselda and Francesca."
For Clifford Bax's Studio Play, " The Rose and The Cross."

AUBREY HAMMOND
" The Lady."
Riding Costume for Ashley Dukes' " The Man With a Load of
Mischief."

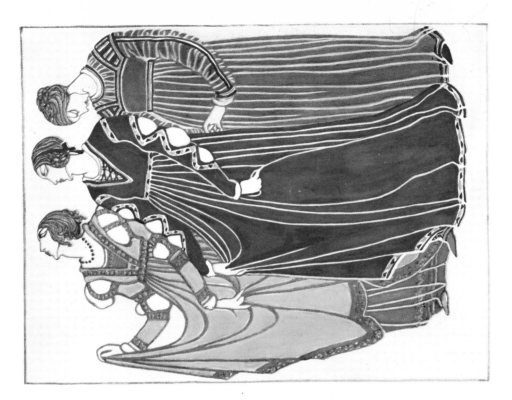

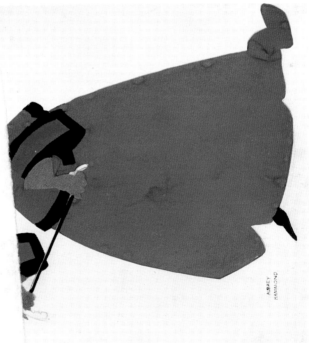

AUBREY
HAMMOND

PLATE CVI

AUBREY HAMMOND
" The Lady."
For Ashley Dukes' " The Man With a Load of Mischief."

"THE MAN WITH A LOAD OF MISCHIEF"

ALTERNATIVE COSTUME
        FOR
    'LADY' (if wearing dark Hair.)
      ACT I.
(BONNET REMOVED ALMOST IMMEDIATELY
    AFTER 1ˢᵗ ENTRANCE)

BLACK CLOAK
WITH 3 CAPES
    FOR
FIRST ENTRANCE →

AUBREY
HAMMOND

(This Costume was used in the Original Production.)

PLATE CVII

GLADYS SPENCER CURLING
" Le Djinne."

PLATE CVIII

DOROTHY MULLOCK
" First and Second Teller."
For Clifford Bax's Studio Play, " The Rose and The Cross."

PLATE CIX

PHILIPPA GEE
" Cleante."
For Moliere's " Le Malade Imaginaire."

CLÉANTE IN
MOLIERE'S
"LE MALADE IMAGINAIRE"

PHILIPPA GEE